CW00406108

LAST GOAL WINS

A History of Football Through Goals

S C CLARKE

INTRODUCTION

If the last scorer of a goal in the first international
football game was to win a title ('The Last Goal
Wins' Trophy) and it created a linear succession
following the below rules, who would be the title
holder, which playing greats and which great games
would it pass through, furthermore, which iconic
goals would be title winners. The rules are : -

*1. The last goalscorer in the game is the holder of
the 'Last Goal Wins' Trophy (starting with the first
international football match).*
*2.The trophy can only be contested when the current
'Last Goal Wins' Trophy holder is playing*
3.Own goals do not count
4.Penalty Shootouts do not count.
*5.Where there is a 0-0 draw, the current title holder
retains their title.*
*6. If the title holder retires, or does not play for
their country again, the title is vacant and
contested in the next match of their country
following the title holder's last game.*

This will be a list showing all title holders up to 1st April 2019. It will also provide a small summary of the player's careers, providing a short history of football through goalscorers, and the goals they scored, the titles they won and the clubs they represented.

The format is as follows : -

number titleholder – player name   country
(number title per country)
match won vs opponent   match score   date

Additional notes : -

Ireland refers to the United Ireland prior to 1921
Eire refers to the Republic of Ireland
Germany, West Germany and East Germany are to deemed to be different entities
The USSR is deemed a different entity to it's successor states.
Yugoslavia is succeeded by Serbia and Montenegro from 2003 to 2006 and then Serbia from 2006 onwards.
Czechoslovakia and it's successor states are deemed to be different entities.

1870 to 1900 –
FOOTBALL'S EARLY YEARS

Unsurprisingly, the 'Last Goal Wins' Trophy remains in the British Isles for football's formative years, as the British 'Home nations would not play against European sides until the early years of the 20th Century. Scotland would dominate the early exchanges in the first international fixtures, with England slowly overtaking the Scottish number of trophies by the end of the century, particularly through the prolific Steve Bloomer.

Countries

England
Scotland
Wales
Ireland

Players

1. Charles Chenery   England (1)

England vs Scotland   4-2   08/03/1873

England's First 'Last Goal Wins' Trophy

Clubs : Crystal Palace, Wanderers.

International Caps / Goals – 3/1

Charles Chenery was the only player to play in the first three international fixtures for England, and scored the final goal in the second international fixture (the first being a 0-0 stalemate). He would later play county cricket also.

2.Angus MacKinnon   Scotland (1)

Scotland vs England   2-1   07/03/1874 (no further appearances for Scotland)

Scotland's First 'Last Goal Wins' Trophy

Clubs : Queens' Park

International Caps / Goals - 1/1

Angus MacKinnon would only play one game for the Scottish national team, scoring the winning goal against England just after half time. The Scottish team of the time was praised for their teamwork and effort against the individually better players of England.

3.Peter Andrews   Scotland (2)

Scotland vs England   2-2   06/03/1875 (no further appearances for Scotland)

Clubs : Glasgow Eastern, Sheffield Heeley

International Caps / Goals – 1/1

Another player who would score in his only game as an international footballer, it is considered that Peter Andrews was the first Scottish player to play his football in England. This goal would come in the 75th minute of the match, suited more to Scotland's passing style of play than the English dribbling.

4. Thomas Highet   Scotland (3)

Scotland vs England   3-0   04/03/1876

Clubs : Queen's Park

International Caps / Goals – 4/1

Thomas Highet's only goal would be a title winner. Like Charles Chenery before him, he would later go on to play cricket. Highet played under the alias of Spencer and sometimes Herriot, for reasons unknown. His son would also represent Queens' Park.

5. Henry McNeil   Scotland (4)

Scotland vs Wales   4-0   25/03/1876

Clubs : Queen's Park, Third Lanark

International Caps / Goals : 10/6

In the first 'Last Goal Wins' Trophy contest which did not include England, Henry McNeil scored in the 70th minute to round off an easy win for the Scotland side. For a period, Henry McNeil was the record holder for international caps.

6. Charles Campbell   Scotland (5)

Scotland vs Wales   2-0   05/03/1877

Clubs: Queen's Park

International Caps/Goals – 13/1

Charles Campbell wasn't the last goalscorer in the game against Wales, but John Smith's own goal would hand Charles the 'Last Goal Wins' Trophy title in Wrexham. Whilst at Queen's Park, Campbell would win eight Scottish Cups and be runner up in two English FA Cups. He would also later serve as President of the Scottish Football Association.

7. Arthur Cursham   England (2)

England vs Scotland   2-7   02/03/1878

Clubs: Notts County

International Caps / Goals : 6/2

Another player who would also play first class cricket, this time for Nottinghamshire and Derbyshire. Cursham would rather tragically die in 1884 of yellow fever in the United States. He is widely believed to have taken the first photograph of an England team.

8. William Henry Davies   Wales (1)

Wales vs England   1-2   18/01/1879

Wales' First 'Last Goal Wins' Trophy

Clubs: Oswestry

International Caps / Goals : 4/1

William Henry Davies would score the first goal for Wales in international football and earn their first 'Last Goal Wins' Trophy, despite being born in Oswestry in England. He would also represent Shropshire at Cricket.

9. John Roberts   Wales (2)

Wales vs England   2-3   15/03/1880

Clubs: Corwen

International Caps / Goals : 7/1

Despite a late consolation for Wales, it would be the next time that these two sides met that the Welsh would finally win an international fixture. Roberts would form part of the first victorious Welsh side, playing his last fixture for Wales in 1883.

10. William Roberts   Wales (3)

Wales vs Scotland   1-5   27/03/1880

Clubs : Llangollen, Crewe Alexandra, Northwich Victoria

International Caps / Goals: 6/2

William Roberts would score a late consolation in a 5-1 hammering by Scotland to maintain Wales hold on the 'Last Goal Wins' Trophy. He would also score against England in the previous fixture before spending the remainder of his career in England.

11. George Ker   Scotland (6)

Scotland vs Wales   5-1   14/03/1881

Clubs: Queens Park, Alexandra Athletic

International Caps / Goals: 5/10

George Ker's astonishing record included two goals against Wales and a hattrick in his next appearance, against England. He gains the 'Last Goal Wins' Trophy on the basis of the fifth Scottish goal being an own goal.

12. John Kay   Scotland (7)

Scotland vs England   5-1   11/03/1882

Clubs : Third Lanark, Queens Park

International Caps / Goals : - 6/5

John Kay would make 6 appearances for Scotland and become the second person to regain the 'Last Goal Wins' Trophy title in 1884 against England. Kay would win three consecutive Scottish cup finals with Queens Park from 1880 to 1882.

13. James McAulay   Scotland (8)

Scotland vs Wales   5-0   25/03/1882

Clubs : Dumbarton

International Caps / Goals: 9/1

James McAuley was ordinarily a goalkeeper, but did occasionally play out of goal, with his only international goal gained him the title. McAulay would win the Scottish cup whilst at Dumbarton and also finish with a runner up medal in his career.

14. John Smith   Scotland (9)

Scotland vs England   3-2   10/03/1883

Clubs : Edinburgh University, Queens' Park, Corinthians

International Caps / Goals : 10/10

John Smith would later represent the British Lions at Rugby Union. He would make his last appearance for the Scottish National football team in 1884, retaining the 'Last Goal Wins' Trophy title, and subsequently being banned from representing Scotland for playing against professionals in England.

15. William Anderson   Scotland (10)

Scotland vs Wales   3-0   12/03/1883

Clubs : Queens Park

International Caps / Goals : 6/3

Anderson would represent Scotland six times, scoring in his final appearance, against Wales in 1885. Anderson would win three Scottish cups with Queen's Park in his career, also finishing with two runners up medals.

16. John Smith   Scotland (11)

Scotland vs England   1-0   15/03/1884 (no further appearances for Scotland)

See Entry 14

17. John Kay   Scotland (12)

Scotland vs Wales   4-1   29/03/1884 (no further appearances for Scotland)

See Entry 12

18. Johnny Gibb   Ireland (1)
Ireland vs   Scotland   2-8   14/03/1885

Ireland's First 'Last Goal Wins' Trophy

Clubs: Cliftonville FC, Wellington Park

International Caps/ Goals : 10/2

The first 'Last Goal Wins' Trophy claimed by Ireland and the first to travel from the island of Great Britain was claimed by a brace from Johnny Gibb for the pre partition Ireland side. His brace in this game would be his only international goals, making his final appearance for Ireland in 1889.

19. Humphrey Jones   Wales (4)

Wales vs   Ireland   8-2   11/04/1885

Clubs : Bangor, East Stirlingshire, Queens Park

International Caps / Goals 14:1

Humphrey would captain Wales in 13 of his 14 appearances, later going on to be a referee at international level. One of the games that he would referee would be the 1896 Home Championship match between Scotland and England.

20. Job Wilding   Wales (5)

Wales vs Ireland   5-0   27/02/1886

Clubs: Everton, Wrexham

International Caps / Goals : - 9/1

Job scored his only international goal in the 1886 Home Nations Championship game against Ireland. Wilding is potentially one of the first professional footballers for Everton, however, his time there was not a successful one, failing to turn up for a fixture for Everton, which forced them to play with nine men.[i]

21. Fred Dewhurst   England (3,4)

England vs   Wales 3-1   29/03/1886 (held for two games)

Clubs : Corinthians, Preston North End
International Caps / Goals : - 9/11

Dewhurst would become the first player to hold the 'Last Goal Wins' Trophy for two consecutive games, and would also score the first Preston North End goal in the Football League. Another who would die young, he passed away in 1895 at the age of 31.

22. Tinsley Lindley   England (5)

England vs Wales   4-0   26/02/1887

Clubs : Nottingham Forest

International Caps / Goals : - 13/14

Tinsley Lindley was a qualified doctor (as was John Smith, **Entry 14**) who would later go on to be rewarded with an OBE for his work in the First World War. Lindley would not wear football boots, rather preferred to wear his walking brogues for football matches.

23. Jimmy Allan   Scotland (13)

Scotland vs England   3-2   19/03/1887 (held for two games, no further appearances)

Clubs : Queens Park

International Caps / Goals : - 2/2

Jimmy Allan would make two appearances for Scotland, clinching the 'Last Goal Wins' Trophy in both with an 80th minute goal against Wales. His goal against England is described as rushing the leather past the keeper in contemporary reports, scoring two minutes after England had equalised.

24. Alex Latta   Scotland (14)

Scotland vs Wales   5-1   10/03/1888

Clubs : Dumbarton, Everton, Liverpool

International Caps / Goals : - 2/2

Latta would begin his youth career at Dumbarton, before moving to Everton as a 14 year old, where he would represent the Liverpool club for six years, winning the English league title in 1891. He would end his career across Stanley Park at Liverpool and retire to start a yacht business.

25. James McLaren   Scotland (15)

Scotland vs England   3-2   13/04/1889

Clubs : Hibernian, Celtic, Greenock Morton, Clyde

International Caps/Goals : - 3/1

James McLaren's last minute winner for Scotland against England in the 1889 Home Championship would be his only goal for Scotland, in a game where he would also captain the side.

26. John McPherson   Scotland (16)

Scotland vs   England   1-1   05/04/1890

Clubs : Kilmarnock, Rangers

International Caps / Goals : - 9/6

McPherson would be a remarkably successful player at Rangers, winning four titles in a row, one of the seasons would be unbeaten. McPherson would score ten goals in his first three games at Rangers. His final appearance for Rangers would come as a goalkeeper, in a 3-2 victory of St. Mirren, securing the title for Rangers.

27. Benjamin Lewis   Wales (6)

Wales vs   Scotland   1-6   26/03/1892

Clubs : Crewe, Chester, Wrexham, Bootle, Middlesbrough.

International Caps/ Goals : 12/4

Benjamin Lewis's 'Last Goal Wins' Trophy would come as an 85th minute consolation against Scotland. He would spend much of his career between Chester and Wrexham, with a season at Middlesbrough sandwiched in the middle of his career.

28.Fred Spiksley   England (6)

England vs   Wales 6-0   13/03/1893 (held for two games)

Clubs : Gainsborough Trinity, Sheffield Wednesday, Leeds City, Watford

International Caps/Goals : - 7/7

Spikesley would go on to be a manager in Sweden, Mexico and Germany, escaping from prison in Germany during the First World War. Spiksley was widely popular in his day, starring on stage with Charlie Chaplin. He would die at Goodwood Racecourse, an irony given his predilection for gambling, in 1948 on Ladies' Day, his bet on the horses' would come through, so a mixed day in all.[ii]

29. William Gibson   Ireland (2)

Ireland vs England 2-2 03/03/1894

Clubs : Cliftonville, Sunderland

International Caps / Goals 14 /1

WK Gibson would later stand for election as a Unionist MP and record the highest number of votes cast in Belfast. His father was an elected fellow of the Royal Society of Antiquaries in Ireland and also vice president of the Irish Football Association.

30.Olphert Stanfield   Ireland (3)

Ireland   vs Scotland   1-2   31/03/1894

Clubs : Genoa, Distillery

International Caps / Goals :- 30/11

Olphie Stanfield was the first Irish footballer to be the top scorer in the Home Nations Championship. Stanfield would be Ireland's record cap holder until 1936 and the World Record Cap holder until 1909.

31.John Goodall   England (7)

England vs   Ireland   9-0   09/03/1895

Clubs : Preston North End, Derby County, New Brighton, Glossop North End, Watford

International Caps / Goals : - 14/12

Goodall would score the second of a brace in a 9-0 hammering of Ireland in the 1895 Home Championships. He would also represent Derbyshire and Hertfordshire at Cricket, and whilst in Hertfordshire, he would become Watford FC's first manager.

32.Steve Smith   England (8)

England vs   Scotland   3-0   06/04/1895 (no further appearances for England)

Clubs : Hednesford Town, Aston Villa, Portsmouth

International Caps/Goals : - 1/1

Smith would score in his only international appearance to gain the 'Last Goal Wins' Trophy. He would be present in five Aston Villa title winning sides before the turn of the century and also win the 1895 FA Cup (although would miss out on the 1897 Villa Cup triumph).

33.Steve Bloomer   England (9,10,11)

England vs   Ireland   2-0   07/03/1896 (held for three games)

Clubs : Derby County, Middlesbrough

International Caps/Goals : - 23/28

Known as the 'Destroying Angel', Steve Bloomer has a phenomenal scoring record at both club and international level, and is also the recipient of the most 'Last Goal Wins' Trophies (9). Another sportsman, he would represent Derby at Baseball also, and later be interned in a German detention camp in the First World War following a spell managing in Berlin. Derby County fans still sing 'Steve Bloomer's Watchin' before every home game.

34.Alf Milward   England (12)

England vs   Wales 4-0   29/03/1897

Clubs : Everton, New Brighton Tower, Southampton

International Caps / Goals : - 4/3

Millward would win titles with Everton and lead Southampton to an FA Cup Final in 1900, despite the Saints being a non-league side at the time. He would also win the English title with Everton in 1891.

35.Jimmy Millar   Scotland (14)

Scotland vs   England   2-1   03/04/1897

Clubs : Sunderland, Rangers

International Caps / Goals : - 3/2

Millar's 83rd minute consolation against England marked a goal on his international debut. He would win four league titles with Sunderland and the 1895 World Championship competed between the English and Scottish Champions. He would also add two Scottish titles to his trophy cabinet with Rangers at the turn of the century.

36.Morgan Morgan-Owen   Wales (7)

Wales vs   Scotland   2-5   19/03/1898

Clubs : Corinthians, Glossop, Nottingham Forest, Casuals

International Caps / Goals : - 12/2

Morgan-Owen would later be awarded for the Distinguished Service Order whilst serving in the First World War seeing action at Gallipoli. He would suffer injury during the war which would bring a close to his football career.

37.Gilbert Smith   England (13)

England vs   Wales 3-0   28/03/1898

Clubs : Oxford University, Old Carthusians, Corinthians

International Caps/ Goals : - 20/11

G.O. Smith is another who would also play first class cricket, this time for Surrey. He is often described as a goal creator and the perfect foil for another 'Last Goal Wins' Trophy recipient, Steve Bloomer. Bloomer and Smith would share the award for the next year.

38.Steve Bloomer   England (14)

England vs   Scotland   3-1   02/04/1898

See Entry 33.

39.Gilbert Smith   England (15)

England vs   Ireland   13-2   13/02/1899

See Entry 37.

40.Steve Bloomer   England (16)

England vs   Wales 4-0   20/03/1899

See Entry 33.

41.Robert Hamilton   Scotland (15)

Scotland vs   England   1-2   08/04/1899

Clubs : Queens Park, Rangers, Fulham, Hearts, Dundee, Elgin City

International Caps/Goals : - 11/15

After retirement, RC Hamilton became a teacher and a key member of the local Elgin community, he would later have a road named after him in Elgin. Hamilton would be Rangers' top scorer for nine consecutive seasons, winning four league titles and two Scottish cups at the club.

1900 to 1918 –
British Isles

The years prior to the First World War would also see the trophy largely change hands between English and Scottish players with Steve Bloomer again prominent. Wales and Ireland would be the other winners, with games being played in the Home Nations Championship taking up much of the international calendar of the time. Many of the winners in this time period would sadly perish in the fighting of the First World War, or come back from the front with injuries that would prevent them from playing football after their experiences in the trenches,

Countries

Scotland
Wales
England
Ireland

<u>Players</u>

42.Alexander Smith   Scotland (16)

Scotland vs Wales   5-2   02/02/1900

Clubs : Rangers

International Caps / Goals: – 20/3

A one club man, Smith would make over 600 competitive appearances for Rangers in his career, in a time that included four consecutive championships. Smith had a reputation as an unselfish player, often working to provide goals for Robert Hamilton (**Entry 41**), although he would be joint top scorer with Hamilton in the 1902 season.

43.John Campbell Scotland (17)

Scotland vs Ireland 3-0   03/03/1900

Clubs: Celtic, Aston Villa, Third Lanark

International Caps/Goals : - 12/4

Campbell won consecutive league titles at Aston Villa and his brace against Ireland in the Home Championships would assist Scotland in winning the competition. Campbell would also win three titles at Celtic and one at Third Lanark during his career in Scotland.

44.Robert McColl   Scotland (18)

Scotland vs England   4-1   07/04/1900

Clubs: Queen's Park, Newcastle United, Rangers

International Caps/Goals : - 13/13

Robert McColl would later set up a newsagent – McColls which remains in operation throughout the United Kingdom. In his last game for Queens Park, McColl would score six goals against Port Glasgow Athletic, who would become defunct shortly afterwards.

45.Thomas Parry Wales (8)

Wales vs Scotland   1-1   02/03/1901

Clubs: Oswestry Town

International Caps / Goals : - 7/3

Parry is from a family of footballers, with brother Maurice also representing Wales and wining two titles with Liverpool, and nephew Frank playing professionally. The two brothers would appear for Wales on four occasions together.

46.Steve Bloomer   (England 17,18)

England vs Wales   6-0   18/03/1901 (held for 2 games)

See Entry 33

47.Jimmy Settle   (England 19)

England vs Ireland   1-0   22/03/1902

Clubs : Bolton Wanderers, Bury, Everton, Stockport County
International Caps : - 6/6

Settle's 18 goal haul in the 1901/1902 season for Everton remains the lowest scoring top flight top scorer levelled only by Dion Dublin , Michael Owen, Jimmy Floyd Hasselbaink and Dwight Yorke in the late nineties.. He would win the FA cup whilst at Everton and post retirement would enter that most ex footballer of careers as a pub landlord.

48.Albert Wilkes   England (20)

England vs Scotland   2-2   03/05/1902 (no further appearances for England)

Clubs : Walsall, West Bromwich Albion, Aston Villa, Fulham
International Caps/Goals : - 5/1

Albert Wilkes' last appearance and only goal for England came in the replayed draw following the Ibrox Disaster of 1902. He would win the title with Aston Villa in two consecutive season and also win the FA Cup in 1905.

49.Henry Davis   England (21)

England vs Ireland   4-0   14/02/1903

Clubs : Barnsley, Sheffield Wednesday
International Caps/ Goals : - 3/1

Davis's goal against Ireland would be his only international goal, and he would shortly win two consecutive league titles with Sheffield Wednesday. Post retirement he would take over a pub in Sheffield which had previously been looked after by William 'Fatty' Foulkes.

50.Vivian Woodward   England (22)

England vs Wales   2-1   02/03/1903

Clubs : Tottenham Hotspur, Chelsea

International Caps/Goals : - 23/29

Woodward's astonishing goalscoring record in international football would last until 1958 following his last England game in 1911. He would serve in the British Army in the First World War, being wounded in 1916. Woodward also has two Olympic gold medals to his name in 1908 and 1912.

51.Bobby Walker Scotland (19)

Scotland vs England   2-1   04/04/1903

Clubs: Heart of Midlothian

International Caps/Goals : - 29/8

Walker is known as one of the most talented footballers of his era, having a cup final named after him in 1901 where he would score the winner and he was the record cap holder for Scotland from 1905 to 1931 and would be the most capped Hearts player for over a hundred years.

52.Bobby Atherton Wales (9)

Wales vs Scotland   1-1   12/03/1904

Clubs : - Heart of Midlothian, Hibernian, Middlesbrough, Chelsea

International Caps/Goals : - 9/2

During the First World War, Atherton would serve as a merchant seaman on the S.S. Britannia which would be lost, presumed sunk by a mine or a submarine. Atherton would captain Hibernian to the Scottish Cup in 1902, a trophy that they would not win again until 2016.

53.Bill McCracken Ireland (4)

Ireland   vs Wales   1-0   21/03/1904

Clubs : Newcastle United

International Caps/Goals : - Ireland 12/1 Northern Ireland 4/0

McCracken's only international goal would not be his greatest contribution to football. His creation of an offside trap led to a change in the rules, making the offside rule require 2 (and not 3) players between the attacker and the goal.[iii]

54.Paddy Sheridan Ireland (5)
Ireland   vs Scotland   1-1   26/03/1904

Clubs : Everton, Stoke, Shelbourne, Accrington Stanley, Hamilton Academical, Clyde, Alloa
International Caps/Goals : - 5/2

James 'Paddy' Sheridan was the first Stoke player to play international football for Ireland. Sheridan would be part of the first Irish side to beat Scotland in 1903, winning the British Home Championships (although joint with England and Scotland) in the process.

55.Steve Bloomer   England (23)
England vs Ireland   1-1   25/02/1905

See Entry 33.

56.Vivian Woodward   England (24)

England vs Wales   3-1   27/03/1905

See Entry 50

57.Joseph Bache   England (25)

England vs Scotland   1-0   01/04/1905

Clubs : Aston Villa, Grimsby Town

International Caps/Goals : - 7/4

Another member of the Aston Villa FA Cup winners of 1905, Bache would not have as much luck in the league, finishing as runner up on five occasions, although would be part of the Villa championship side of 1910. Bache is another who would later join the war effort, surviving the Western Front and becoming a Lance-Corporal. Following the war he would become a pub landlord and coach in Germany.

58.Harold Hardman   England (26)

England vs Ireland 1-0   16/02/1907

Clubs : Blackpool, Everton, Manchester United, Bradford City, Stoke City

International Caps/Goals : - 4/1

Hardman would win the FA Cup at Everton in 1906, before signing for Manchester United in 1908 and finishing his law degree. Upon retirement, Hardman would become a solicitor, following in his father's footsteps and later be Chairman for Manchester United at the time of the Munich Air Disaster.

59.Steve Bloomer   England (27)

England vs Scotland   1-1   06/04/1907 (no further appearances for England)

See Entry 33

60.George Hilsdon England (28)
England vs Ireland 3-1   15/02/1908

Clubs : West Ham, Chelsea

International Caps / Goals : - 8/14

Hilsdon's would be part of the 1909 British Home Championship winning side for England and would receive two runners up medals for the English Second Division. He would survive the First World War, but the damage sustained to his lungs in a gas attack in Arras in 1917 would end his football career.

61.Tinker Davies Wales (10)

Wales vs England   1-7   16/03/1908

Clubs : Wrexham, Blackburn

International Caps/Goals : - 11/5

William 'Tinker' Davies was known so due to his training as a tinsmith. In his career, Davies would win the Welsh Cup twice with Wrexham and the English title with Blackburn Rovers. He would also survive the war, having served in Malta.

62.Harold Paul Scotland (20)

Scotland vs Wales   3-2   01/03/1909 (held for 2 games)

Clubs : Queen's Park

International Caps/Goals – 3/2

Both of Paul's goals would be 'Last Goal Wins' Trophy winners. Paul would become a vet before enlisting in the war effort as part of the Royal Army Veterinary Corps before returning to his career as a veterinary surgeon.

63.George Wall   England (29)

England vs Scotland   2-0   03/04/1909

Clubs : Barnsley, Manchester United, Cowdenbeath, Oldham, Hamilton Academical, Rochdale

International Caps/Goals : - 7/2

Wall would win two league titles and an FA Cup during his time at Manchester United, also having his career interrupted by the war where he served in the Black Watch regiment on the Western Front.

64.Andrew Ducat   England (30)

England vs Wales   1-0   14/03/1910

Clubs : Southend, Arsenal, Aston Villa, Fulham

International Caps / Goals : - 3/1

Ducat would also represent England at international cricket in one test against Australia and would die in a cricket match at Lords in 1942 from heart failure. Ducat would win one FA Cup in his time at Arsenal.

65.James Quinn Scotland (21)

Scotland vs England   2-0   02/04/1910 (held for 2 games)

Clubs : Celtic

International Caps/Goals :- 11/7

Quinn is still the second highest league scorer in Celtic's history and his grandson would also play for Celtic. His time at the Glasgow club would see them win six Scottish titles and five Scottish cups.

66.George Holley   England (31)

England vs Scotland   1-1   23/03/1912

Clubs : Sunderland, Brighton
International Caps/Goals : - 10/8

Holley was the top scorer in the 1911/12 season of the First Division and would score in
all three games of the 1912 Home Championships. He would win the English Title with Sunderland in 1913 and his son would also be a professional footballer, playing for Barnsley and Leeds.

67.Harry Hampton England (32)

England vs Scotland   1-0   05/04/1913

Clubs : Aston Villa, Birmingham, Newport County
International Caps/Goals : - 4/2

Hampton remains the leading league scorer for Aston Villa to this day and scored both goals in the 1905 FA Cup final, which would be won again in 1913 with Aston Villa. Like Joe Bache (**Entry 57),** Hampton would finish as runner up in the English League on 5 occassions, winning the title only once in 1909. Hampton would also become a pub landlord.

68.Billy Wedlock   England (33)

England vs Wales   2-0   16/03/1914 (no further appearances for England)

Clubs : Bristol City

International Caps/Goals : - 26/2

Wedlock would be part of Bristol City's most successful era, winning the second tier in England, and finishing as runners up in both the top flight and FA Cup, and subsequently a stand would be named after him at Bristol City's Ashton Gate until it's redevelopment in 2014. He would also become a pub landlord.

69.William Reid Scotland (22)

Scotland vs England   3-1   04/04/1914 (no further appearances for Scotland)

Clubs : Morton, Third Lanark, Motherwell, Portsmouth, Rangers, Albion Rovers

International Caps/Goals : - 9/4

Reid's international career would be halted by the First World War like many of his era, he would return from duty, but didn't make further international appearances. Reid would be win three consecutive titles with Rangers from 1910 to 1913, and finish as top goalscorer in two of those season. He remains the fourth top goalscorer in the Scottish top flight.

1918 – 1946
How Dare They Play Our Game!

The broadening of international football following the First World War and the beginning of the end of the reluctance of the 'Home Nations' to play their European counterparts, the trophy becomes more widespread taking in much of the great Central European teams of the era and even making a short stop across the Atlantic in Brazil. The trophy would remain in the hands of the neutral and Axis powers during the Second World War, meaning that it would be competed throughout the conflict. The changing of borders throughout the era and the creation of new countries and population transfers would see the first players win the trophy for multiple countries.

Countries

Scotland
Wales
England
Belgium
Austria
Czechoslovakia
Hungary
Italy
Netherlands
Eire

Spain
Brazil
Yugoslavia
Greece
Romania
Switzerland
Germany

Players

70.Tommy Cairns Scotland (23)

Scotland vs Wales   1-1   26/02/1920

Clubs : Bristol City, St Johnstone, Rangers, Bradford City

International Caps/Goals : 8/1

Cairns would never lose in his short international career and would score his only goal as an equaliser against Wales. Cairns would spend fourteen years at Rangers, winning the league title in seven of those seasons, eventually retiring at Bradford at the age of 42.

71. Andrew Wilson Scotland (24,25,26,27)

Scotland vs England   1-0   08/04/1922 (held for 4 games)

Clubs : - Middlesbrough, Dunfermline, Chelsea, QPR, SC Nimois, Hearts

International Caps/ Goals : - 12/13

In spite of having his forearm shattered in France during the First World War, Wilson would become a prolific goalscorer for club and country. Wilson's goalscoring would lead Scotland to the British Home Championships three times in a row.

72.Len Davies Wales (11)

Wales vs Scotland   2-0   16/02/1924

Clubs : Cardiff City, Bangor City

International Caps/Goals : - 23/6

Davies remains the top scorer in all competitions for Cardiff City and would win the FA Cup and Welsh Cup with the side. Davie's missed penalty in the 1923-24 season would ensure that Huddersfield Town won the title on goal average, by 0.024 of a goal.

73.Ted Vizard Wales (12)

Wales vs England   2-1   03/03/1924

Clubs : Barry, Bolton Wanderers

International Caps/Goals : - 22/1

Vizard would win three FA Cups with Bolton Wanderers during his 21 year stint at the club. Vizard would manage Swindon Town, QPR (where the Second World War would prevent him from managing a single competitive game) and Wolverhampton Wanderers following retirement.

74.Moses Russell Wales (13)

Wales vs Northern Ireland 1-0   15/03/1924

Clubs : Ton Pentre, Merthyr Town, Plymouth Argyle, Llanelli
International Caps/Goals : - 23/1

Russells' penalty against Northern Ireland would be his only international goal although would not be his most notable penalty. During a tour of Argentina, in an event to quell crowd trouble, Russell's Plymouth Argyle teammates decided to miss a penalty, Russell would not have this, and stepped up and smashed the ball in the back of the net to the anger of the crowd.

75.Hughie Gallacher   Scotland (28)

Scotland vs Wales   3-1   14/02/1925

Clubs : Queen of the South, Airdrieonians, Newcastle, Chelsea, Derby County, Notts County, Grimsby Town, Gateshead

International Caps/Goals : 20/24

Gallacher's outstanding career and goal scoring record would be overshadowed by his tragic death. Facing trial for a domestic assault on his son, Gallacher decided to take his own life on the railway tracks in Gateshead. Only two players have scored more goals than Gallacher at international level for Scotland.

76.James Dunn Scotland (29)

Scotland vs Northern Ireland   3-0   28/02/1925

Clubs : - Hibernian, Everton, Exeter City, Runcorn

International Caps/Goals : - 6/2

Dunn would win the English Second Division and First Division in successive seasons at Everton from 1930-1932 and also the FA Cup in 1933. His son Jimmy Dunn Jr. would also win the FA Cup in 1949.

77.Alan Morton   Scotland (30)

Scotland vs Northern Ireland   2-0   26/02/1927

Clubs : Queen's Park, Rangers

International Caps/Goals : - 31/5

Morton would create three of the goals in the 5-1 defeat of England by the Scottish 'Wembley Wizards' and a portrait of Morton remains at Ibrox reflecting his long association with Rangers, a club where he won ten Scottish league titles.

78.Dixie Dean   England (34)

England vs   Scotland   2-1   02/04/1927

Clubs : - Tranmere Rovers, Everton, Notts County, Sligo Rovers
International Caps/Goals : - 16/18

Dean would have astonishing goal scoring exploits in the 1927/28 season with 60 goals scored. To this day, only one player has scored more English league goals than Dean. Dean would win two league titles and a Second Division championship at Everton, along with the FA Cup in 1933. He would also become a pub landlord.

79.Florimond van Halme   Belgium (1)

Belgium vs England1-9   11/05/1927

Belgium's First 'Last Goal Wins' Trophy – First title outside of the British Isles

Clubs: Cercle Brugge

International Caps/Goals : - 39/2

Vanhalme would be the first player from outside of the British Isles to win the trophy with a consolation goal in a 9-1 hammering by England. Spending his entire career at Cercle Brugge, he would win the Belgian title twice and represent his country in the 1924 and 1928 Olympics.

80.Anton Schall   Austria (1)

Austria   vs Belgium 4-1   22/05/1927

Austria's First 'Last Goal Wins' Trophy

Clubs : Admira Vienna

International Caps / Goals : - 28/27

Schall would form part of the Austrian side which finished 4th in the 1934 World Cup. He would die whilst coach of FC Basel in Switzerland having led them to the Swiss Cup in his first season in charge.

81.Josef Silny   Czechoslovakia (1)

Czechoslovakia vs Austria 1-0   01/04/1928

Czechoslovakia's First 'Last Goal Wins' Trophy

Clubs : Slavia Prague, Sparta Prague, SC Nimois, Bohemians, Slavia Kroměříž

International Caps / Goals : - 50/28

The scorer of Czechoslovakia's first 'Last Goal Wins' Trophy, Silny would also be part of the squad which finished as runners up in the 1934 World Cup. He would win three Czechoslovak titles during his career, one at Slavia Prague and two at Sparta.

82. Vilmos Kohut   Hungary (1)

Hungary vs Czechoslovakia   2-0   22/04/1928

Hungary's First 'Last Goal Wins' Trophy

Clubs : Ferencvaros, Marseille, Nimes, Antibes

International Caps/ Goals : - 25/14

Kohut would finish with a runner up medal at the 1938 World Cup for the Hungarian national side and would win the Mitropa Cup in 1928, an early Central European international club competition. He would win three titles in Hungary and one in France, along with two French cups.

83.Ferdinand Wesely Austria (2)

Austria   vs Hungary 5-5   06/05/1928

Clubs : Rapid Vienna, St Gallen, FC Basel, Nordstern Basel

International Caps/Goals : - 40/17

Wesely would captain Rapid to the 1930s Mitropa Cup, a forerunner of modern European Club tournaments. Whilst at Rapid Vienna, he would also win four Austrian titles and one Austrian Cup, adding a Swiss Cup with Basel later in his career.

84.Rudolf Seidl Austria (3)

Austria   vs Sweden   3-2   29/07/1928 (no further games for Austria)

Clubs : Austria Vienna, First Vienna

International Caps/Goals : - 8/1

Seidl last involvement for Austria would be this winner against Sweden. He would win two titles for First Vienna and would later return to both of his clubs to manage them in the 1930s.

85.Fritz Gschweidl Austria (4)

Austria   vs Hungary 5-1   07/10/1928

Clubs : First Vienna

International Caps / Goals : - 44/12

Freidrich 'Fritz' Gschweidl would win five Austrian titles and three cups in his career at First Vienna. He would not form a part of the Austrian fourth place finish in the 1934 World Cup despite being an integral part of the 'Wunderteam' in the years' preceding.

86.Hans Tandler Austria (5)

Austria   vs Switzerland   2-0   28/10/1928

Clubs – Vienna Cricket and Football Club, SV Amateure, New York Giants, Austria Vienna

International Caps/Goals : - 18/3

Tandler would join several high profile players in joining New York Giants in the United States including Bela Guttman, later known for his 'curse' on Benfica. Whilst in Austria, he would win the Austrian title on two occasions and be a three time Austrian Cup winner.

87.Leopoldi Conti Italy (1)

Italy vs Austria   2-2   11/11/1928

Italy's First 'Last Goal Wins' Trophy

Clubs : Internazionale, Padova, Pro Patria

International Caps/Goals : - 31/8

Conti would be captain of Internazionale for nine years from 1922 to 1931 before leaving for Pro Patria, leading them to two titles. Internationally, he would represent Italy in the 1924 Olympic Games in Paris.

88.Adolfo Baloncieri Italy (2)

Italy vs Netherlands   3-2   02/12/1928

Clubs : Alessandria, Torino, Comense

International Caps/Goals : - 47/25

Baloncieri played in three Olympic Games and remains the highest scoring midfielder for the Italian national team and the sixth highest scorer overall. Following retirement from the playing field, he would turn his hand to management, taking charge of several teams until his complete retirement in 1962

89.Marcello Mihalich   Italy (3)

Italy vs Portugal   6-1   01/12/1929 (no further appearances for Italy)

Clubs : Fiumana, Napoli, Ambrosiana-Inter, Juventus, Pistoiese, Catania

International Caps/Goals : 1 / 2

Born in what is now Rijeka, Croatia, Mihalich's only cap saw him score twice. His one season at Juventus would yield a Serie A championship. Mihalich would be the first Napoli player to play for the Italian national team.

90.Giuseppe Meazza Italy (4,5)

Italy vs Switzerland 4-2   09/02/1930 (held for 2 games)

Clubs : Internazionale, Milan, Juventus, Varese, Atalanta

International Caps / Goals : - 53/33

Meazza had a storied and illustrious career playing for both Milan sides, winning the World Cup twice and having the San Siro stadium in Milan named for him. He remains the fourth highest scorer in Serie A history, and the second highest scorer for the Italian national team. A prolific scorer, Meazza enjoyed the high life of champagne and cigars, and would allegedly sleep in a brothel before matches.

91.Jan van den Broek   Netherlands (1)

Netherlands vs Italy   1-1   06/04/1930

Netherlands First 'Last Goal Wins' Trophy

Clubs : Breda, PSV

International Caps/Goals : - 11/4

Van den Broek was originally from Breda, and would move to PSV Eindhoven in 1927, when he would win his first international cap for his country. He would win two titles with PSV in 1929 and 1935.

92.Ferdinand Adams Belgium (2)

Belgium vs Netherlands   2-2   04/05/1930

Clubs : Anderlecht

International Caps/Goals : - 23/9

Adams formed part of the Belgian side that travelled to Uruguay for the first World Cup. He retired age 30 due to muscle injuries after 15 years at Anderlecht. He would die on Christmas Day 1985 at the age of 82 years old.

93.John Joe Flood   Eire (1)

Eire vs Belgium   3-1   11/05/1930

Eire's First 'Last Goal Wins' Trophy

Clubs : Shamrock Rovers, Shelbourne, Leeds, Crystal Palace, Reds United

International Caps/ Goals : - 5/4

Ireland's first 'Last Goal Wins' Trophy as an independent nation would be scored by Flood. Flood was very successful in Irish football, being part of four League of Ireland title winning sides, and a total of six Irish cups.

94. Angel Arocha   Spain (1)

Spain vs Eire 1-1   26/04/1931

Spain's First 'Last Goal Wins' Trophy

Clubs : Tenerife, Barcelona, Atletico Madrid

International Caps/Goals : - 2/2

Arocha would score nearly a goal a game whilst at Barcelona, leading the club to the 1929 title and 1928 Spanish Cup. The outbreak of the Spanish Civil War would end his career, and he would die whilst fighting for the Francoist army in 1938.

95.Marti Vantolra Spain (2)

Spain vs Eire 5-0   13/12/1931

Clubs : Espanyol, Sevilla, Barcelona, Real Club Espana, Atlante

International Caps / Goals : - 12/3

Ventolra would flee Spain during the Spanish Civil War to Mexico, where he would continue his career. His son would win thirty caps for Mexico and both father and son would play in World Cups (Marti in 1934, his son Jose in 1970).

96.Isidro Langara Spain (3,4)

Spain vs Portugal   9-0   11/03/1934 (held for 2 games)

Clubs : Oviedo, CD Euskadi, San Lorenzo de Almagro, Real Club Espana

International Caps / Goals : - 12 /17

Another player affected by the Civil War, Langara would flee Spain to play for the Basque 'national team' in Mexico and Argentina. He did return to Spain towards the end of his career, but left for South America after a single season.

97.Leonidas   Brazil (1)

Brazil vs Spain   3-1   27/05/1934

Brazil's First 'Last Goal Wins' Trophy – First 'Last Goal Wins' Trophy outside Europe, First 'Last Goal Wins' Trophy in South America

Clubs : - Bonsuccesso, Penarol, Vasco da Gama, Botafogo, Flamengo, Sao Paulo
International Caps / Goals : - 19/21

Leonidas played in both the 1934 and 1938 World Cups for Brazil and subsequently had a chocolate bar named for him – which remains popular in Brazil. Leonidas is possibly the inventor of the bicycle kick and performed one in the 1938 World Cup where he would win the Golden Boot as top scorer and help Brazil to third place.

98.Blagoje Marjanovic Yugoslavia (1,2)

Yugoslavia vs Brazil   8-4   03/06/1934 (held for 2 games)

Yugoslavia's First 'Last Goal Wins' Trophy

Clubs : Jugoslavija, SK Olimpija, BSK Beograd, Cukaricki, Dinamo Pancevo, Proleter Osijek

International Caps / Goals : - 58/37

Marjanovic would win six Yugoslav championships and represent his country in the 1930 World Cup, where they would finish in third place. Later, he would be captured in the Second World War invasion of Yugoslavia and taken to a prison camp in Germany.

99.Branislav Sekulic Yugoslavia (3)

Yugoslavia vs   Czechoslovakia   1-3
          02/09/1934

Clubs : Jugoslavija, Montpellier, Club Francais, Grasshoppers, Urania Geneva, Jedinstvo Beograd

International Caps / Goals : - 17/8

Another member of the Yugoslav squad that reached the semi finals of the 1930 World Cup, Sekulic would also win two Yugoslav championships in his career. Following the Second World War, he would return to Switzerland where he spent several years of his playing career, to manage the national team.

100.Leonidas Andrianopoulos   Greece (1)

Greece   vs Yugoslavia   2-1
        23/12/1934

Greece's First 'Last Goal Wins' Trophy

Clubs : - Olympiacos

International Caps / Goals : - 11/2

Andrianapoulos would play at Olympiacos with four of his brothers, winning the Greek title on three occasions with the Piraeus club. He would live to the age of 100, dying in October 2011.

101.Kostas Choumis Greece (2)

Greece   vs Romania 2-2   27/12/1934

Clubs : Ethnikos Piraeus, Venus Bucuresti, Karres Medias, IT Arad

International Caps/Goals : - Greece 9/7 Romania 2/1

Choumis would move to Romania in 1935 following the two countries fixture in 1935. He would later represent them internationally after spending several years in the country at Venus Bucuresti.

102.Iuliu Bodola Romania (1)

Romania vs Greece 5-2   17/05/1936

Romania's First 'Last Goal Wins' Trophy

Clubs : CA Oaradea, Venus Bucuresti, Nagyvaradi AC, Ferar Cluj, MTK Hungaria

International Caps/Goals : - Romania 48/30 Hungary 13/4

Bodola would also represent two countries in his career, seeing out his career and settling in Hungary. His son would become a famous Hungarian illustrator. He would also gain a 'Last Goal Wins' Trophy for Hungary, becoming the first player to do so for two countries.

103.Stefan Dobay Romania (2)

Romania vs Bulgaria   4-1   24/05/1936

Clubs : Banatul Timisoara, Ripensia Timisoara, CA Cluj, Torekves SE, Flacara Medias
International Caps/Goals : - 41/9

Dobay would represent Romania at both the 1934 and 1938 World Cups, scoring in both competitions. Whilst at Ripensia Timisoara he would be top scorer in the Romanian League for four seasons and win the league title on four occasions also.

104.Geza Toldi Hungary (2)

Hungary vs Romania   2-1   04/10/1936

Clubs : Ferencvaros, Gamma FC, Szegedi AK, Zugloi Madisz

International Caps/Goals : - 46/25

Toldi would represent Hungary in two World Cups in 1934 and 1938, captaining his country for a period in between. Upon retirement, Toldi would have a storied managerial career in Denmark and Belgium, winning the double with Aarhus in 1960 and also becoming manager of the Belgium national team in the 1950s.

105.Vlastimil Kopecky   Czechoslovakia (2)

Czechoslovakia vs Hungary   5-2   18/10/1936

Clubs : Rapid Vinohrady, Slavia Prague

International Caps / Goals : - 26/8

Kopecky is the second highest goalscorer in Czech league history and took part in both the 1934 and 1938 World Cups. He would five Czechoslovak titles including one after the Second World War, and win four titles under German Occupation also.

106.Fredy Bickel   Switzerland (1)

Switzerland vs Czechoslovakia   3-5   21/02/1937

Switzerland's First 'Last Goal Wins' Trophy

Clubs : Grasshoppers Zurich

International Caps Goals : - 71/5

Bickel is one of only two players to appear in World Cups before and after the Second World War. A one club man, Bickel would win seven titles in his twenty one year spell at Grasshoppers Zurich and would manage them twice, having a twenty nine year association with the club.

107.Max Abegglen Switzerland (2)

Switzerland vs Netherlands   1-2   07/03/1937

Clubs : FC Cantonal, Lausanne Sports, Grasshopper Zurich

International Caps/Goals : 68/34

The Swiss Club, Neuchatel Xamax is named for Max Abegglen and he was the Swiss national team's top scorer until 2008, when overtaken by Alexander Frei. Abegglen would represent Switzerland with two of his brothers and would take part in the 1924 Olympic Games, unfortunately, missing the 1934 World Cup.

108.Janos Dudas   Hungary (3)

Hungary vs Switzerland   5-2   11/04/1937

Clubs : MTK Budapest, Csepel SC

International Caps/Goals : - 21/3

Dudas would represent his country in both the 1934 and 1938 World Cups, finishing runner up in the latter. He would win four Hungarian titles in his career, two of which were during the Second World War.

109.Gyorgy Sarosi   Hungary (4)

Hungary vs Czechoslovakia   8-3   19/09/1937

Clubs : Ferencvaros

International Caps/Goals : - 62/42

Sarosi would score nearly a goal a game at Ferencvaros and was named in the top 100 European players of the 20th Century by the International Federation of Football History and Statistics[iv]. At domestic level, he would win five titles in Hungary, and in his post playing days would manage Juventus to a Serie A title in 1952.

110.Laszlo Cseh   Hungary (5)

Hungary vs Austria 2-1   10/10/1937

Clubs : MTK Hungaria, Kispesti, Szegedi AK, Gamma FC

International Caps/Goals : - 34/15

Cseh would form part of the 1938 Hungarian World Cup squad but would not make an appearance in the finals. Laszlo Cseh shares his name with two Hungarian Olympic swimmers, also known as Laszlo Cseh.

111.Gyorgy Sarosi   Hungary (6)

Hungary vs Scotland   1-3   07/12/1938

See Entry 109

112.Bertus de Harder   Netherlands (2)

Netherlands vs Hungary   2-3   26/02/1939

Clubs : Den Haag, Girondins de Bordeaux, Holland Sport, AS Angouleme

International Caps/Goals : 11/3

De Harder would have greater success in his career upon moving to France, winning the title and finishing as top scorer for Bordeaux in 1950. He would return to Netherlands only to end his career in France and take up management in the country.

113.Jean Capelle   Belgium (3)

Belgium vs Netherlands   5-4   19/03/1939

Clubs : Standard Liege

International Caps/Goals : - 34/19

Capelle would score 245 goals in 285 appearances for Standard Liege and would play in both the 1934 and 1938 World Cups. He remains one of the youngest players to play for the Belgian national team having made his debut at the age of 17 years and 153 days.

114.Leen Vente   Netherlands (3)

Netherlands vs Belgium   3-2   23/04/1939

Clubs : Neptunus, Feyenord

International Caps/Goals : - 21/19

Another who would appear for his country in both 1934 and the 1938 World Cups, Vente score the first goal in Feyenoord's De Kuip stadium and his great nephew currently plays for the club where Leen Vente won two titles.

115.Lauro Amado Switzerland (3,4,5)

Switzerland vs Netherlands   2-1   07/05/1939
(held for 3 games)

Clubs : Lugano, Servette, Grasshoppers Zurich
International Caps/Goals : - 54/21

Amado would play in the 1938 World Cup and is the first holder of the 'Last Goal Wins' Trophy for more than two games since the early nineteen twenties. Amado would win five titles in Switzerland and also five Swiss cups.

116.Georges Aeby Switzerland (6)

Switzerland vs Italy 3-1   12/11/1939

Clubs : FC Biel Bienne, Servette FC, FC Lausanne Sport, Urania Geneve Sport

International Caps / Goals : 39/13

Aeby's brother Paul also played for the Swiss national team twenty times in this era and both would represent Switzerland in the 1938 World Cup. Aeby would be top scorer in the Swiss top flight in 1940.

117.Guido Corbelli Italy (6)

Italy vs Switzerland 1-1   03/03/1940 (no further appearances for Italy)

Clubs : Sassuolo, Carpi, Anconitana, Venezia, Atalanta, Milan, Parma, Cesena, Cosenza

International Caps / Goals : 1/1

Corbelli spent much of his career in the lower leagues of Italian football, winning Serie C with Anconitana before getting a chance in Serie A with Venezia, Milan and Atlanta during the Second Wolrd War.

118.Amedeo Biavati   Italy (7)

Italy vs Germany   3-2   05/04/1940

Clubs : Bologna, Catania, Reggina, Imolese, Magenta, Belluno
International Caps/Goals : - 18/8

Biavati would win Serie A three times with Bologna and be part of the Italian World Cup winning side of 1938. He is widely believed to have popularised the step over in Italy and was famous for his skills on the wing.

119.Silvio Piola   Italy (8)

Italy vs Romania   2-1   14/04/1940

Clubs : Pro Vercelli, Lazio, Torino, Juventus, Novara
International Caps / Goals : - 34/30

Piola won the World Cup with Italy in 1938 but would not play in 1950, despite still playing international football, as he was not selected in Italy's squad for the tournament. Piola remains the highest scorer in Serie A history. His final appearance would be against England in 1952, an opponent whom he scored with a handball against in 1939.

120.Iuliu Bodola   Hungary (7)

Hungary vs Italy   1-1   01/12/1940

See entry 102

121.Ferenc Sarvari   Hungary (8)
Hungary vs Croatia 1-1   08/12/1940

Clubs : CA Oradea, UD Resita, Nagyvaradi AC, IC Oradea, Mel
International Caps/Goals : - Romania 11/4
Hungary 7/3

Another who would represent both Romania and Hungary in his international career, Sarvari was also known as Francisc Spielmann. Interestingly, Sarvari would live in and play football in both the Hungarian and Romanian league for the same side – Oradea (or Nagyvaradi in Hungarian) becoming part of Hungary as part of the Second Vienna Award in 1940.

122.Numa Monnard   Switzerland (7)

Switzerland vs Hungary   1-2   16/11/1941

Clubs : - Neuchatel, Basel, Lausanne

International Caps / Goals : - 15/6

Numa Monnard would make his international debut against Belgium in 1936 and due to Switzerland's neutrality in the Second World War, continue his career throughout. He would be top scorer in the Swiss league in 1938.

123.Rodolfo Kappenberger   Switzerland (8,9)

Switzerland vs Germany   2-1   01/02/1942 (held for 2 games)

Clubs : - SC Zug, FC Lugano, FC Basel

International Caps/ Goals : - 6/5

All of Kappenberger's caps would come during the Second World War where Switzerland maintained fixtures against the Axis nations. He would win one Swiss title in this period with Lugano and win the Swiss cup with Basel in 1947.

124.Fritz Walter   Germany (1)
Germany vs Switzerland   5-3   18/10/1942

Germany's First 'Last Goal Wins' Trophy

Clubs : Kaiserslautern
International Caps / Goals : - 61/33

Walter would captain West Germany to the 1954
World Cup and have Kaiserslautern's stadium
named for him. After catching malaria in the Second
World War, he struggled to play well in heat with
the phrase 'Fritz Walter's weather' to describe rain
being taken into the German language. Walter
would have a lucky escape in the Second World
War when the Soviet Army captured him, it is said
that a Hungarian guard recognised his footballing
history and advised the Soviets that he was not
German, thus potentially saving his life.

125.August Klingler   Germany (2)

Germany vs Croatia 5-1   01/11/1942

Clubs : - FV Daxlanden
International Caps/Goals : 5/6

Klingler would not have the luck of Fritz Walter in
the Second World War, dying on the Eastern Front
at the age of 26. His international appearances
would all come during the Second World War,
scoring a hat trick in Germany's last fixture until
1950 against Slovakia.

126.Karl Decker   Germany (3)

Germany vs Slovakia   5-2   22/11/1942

Clubs : - First Vienna, Sturm Graz, Sochauz, Grenchen

International Caps/Goals : - Germany 8/8 Austria 25/19

Decker's stints at his first two clubs, First Vienna and Sturm Graz would see him score more than a goal a game. Born in Austria, Decker would represent Germany following Anschluss. Karl Decker's next international appearance was for Austria following the division of the two countries and their occupation by the allied powers at the end of the Second World War. He would win the 'Last Goal Wins' Trophy whilst representing Austria also.

127.Gyula Zsengeller   Hungary (9)

Hungary vs Austria 2-0   19/08/1945

Clubs : Salgotarjani, Ujpest FC, AS Roma, AC Ancona, Deportivo Samarios

International Caps / Goals : - 39/33

Zsengeller is another who averaged over a goal a game – notably in his time at Ujpest where he would score 368 goals in 301 games. He would end his career in Colombia, before embarking on a managerial career in Italy and Cyprus. Zsengeller would be top scorer in the Hungarian league for five seasons.

128.Ferenc Szusza   Hungary (10)

Hungary vs Austria 5-2   20/08/1945

Clubs : Ujpesti Dosza

International Caps / Goals : 24/18

Szusza had scored more league goals for one club than any other player in history until Lionel Messi overtook him in the 2018/2019 season. He would the Hungarian title with Ujpest on four occasions, and his post playing career would see him manage in Hungary, Poland and Real Betis and Atletico Madrid in Spain.

1946 to 1960
THE NEWISH WORLD - SOUTH AMERICA

The post war period would see the 'Last Goal Wins' Trophy dominated by South American players, with the European sides meeting them in the 1950 World Cup and relinquishing the trophy, where Ghiggia's goal in the Maracana would be a winner of the 'Last Goal Wins' Trophy and a World Cup winning goal. It would not return to Europe until 1958 during the World Cup in Sweden.

Countries

Austria
France
England
Switzerland
Belgium
Netherlands
Wales
Spain
Uruguay
Brazil
Bolivia
Chile
Peru
Argentina

West Germany

Players

129. Karl Decker   Austria (6)

Austria vs Hungary 3-2   14/04/1946

See Entry 125.

130.Lucien Le Duc France (1)
France vs Austria   3-1   05/05/1946 (no further
appearances for France)

France's First 'Last Goal Wins' Trophy

Clubs : - Boulougne, Montpellier, Sete, Clermont,
Red Star Saint-Ouen, CO Roubaix Tourcoing, RC
Paris, SSC Venezia, Saint Etienne, FC Annecy

International Caps/ Goals : - 4/1

Le Duc's only international goal would see him gain
the trophy. He ended a 47 year career in football
managing Paris Saint Germain in 1984. He would
win one French title as a player in 1947 and four as a
manager (three with Monaco and one with
Marseille)

131.Rene Bihel France (2)

France vs Portugal   1-0   23/03/1947 (no further apperances for France)

Clubs : Valenciennes, Le Havre, Lille, Marseille, Toulon, Strasbourg

International Caps / Goals : - 6/1

Bihel was nicknamed the Norman Bull and would later also coach Le Havre, who he played for on three separate occasions. He would win the French title with Lille in 1946 whilst finishing as top scorer in the division, and also add to that with a title in 1948 with Marseille.

132.Raich Carter   England (35)

England vs France   3-0   03/05/1947

Clubs :- Sunderland, Derby County, Hull City, Cork Athletic

International Caps/Goals : – 13/7

Another who would play county cricket, Carter is the only player to win FA Cup medals before and after the Second World War and was, at the time, the youngest captain to lead his team to the championship in England following Sunderland's triumph in 1936.

133.Jacques Fatton Switzerland (10)

Switzerland vs England   1-0   18/05/1947

Clubs : Servette, Lyon

International Caps / Goals : - 53/28

Fatton was originally born in France and would represent Switzerland in two World Cups, scoring in both. Domestically, he would win four titles with Servette and finish as top scorer in the Swiss League on three separate occasions, in 1949, 1950 and 1962.

134.Jean Baratte   France (3)

Francevs Switzerland   2-1   08/06/1947

Clubs: Olympique Lillois, Lille Flandres, Lille, AS Aix, CO Roubaix-Tourcoing

International Caps/Goals : - 32/19

Baratte was nicknamed ' Captain Courageous' in his time at Lille, leading the side to two titles and four French Cups during his time there. He would go on to manage Lille for on season, whilst also managing in Tunisia at ES Tunis

135. Larbi Benbarek   France (4)

France vs Portugal 4-2   23/11/1947

Clubs : Ideal Club Casablanca, US Marocaine, Marseille, Stade Francais, Atletico Madrid, USM Bel Abbes

International Caps / Goals :- 19/3

Benbarek is considered one of the first successful African footballers in European football, having been born and raised in Morocco. He took the nickname 'Black Pearl' which would be later adopted by Pele, an admirer of the player. He would win two titles with Atletico Madrid in Spain and despite only making 19 appearances for the French national team, would see his international career span nearly 16 years.

136.Jean Baratte France (5,6)

France vs Italy   1-3   04/04/1948 (held for 2 games)

See Entry 134

137.Fredy Chaves Belgium (4,5)

Belgium vs France   4-2   06/06/1948 (held for 2 games)

Clubs : La Gantoise, Waregem, Kortrijk, KRC Gent Zeehaven

International Caps / Goals : - 20/8

Chaves would also coach Waregem on two occasions, having a total of four spells at the club. Chaves would captain the Belgian national between 1949 and 1951 and his career in football would eventually finish in 1972.

138.Mick Clavan   Netherlands (4)

Netherlands vs Belgium   1-1   21/11/1948

Clubs : - ADO, SHS, Holland Sport

International Caps/Goals : - 27/7

Despite winning only 27 caps, Clavan's international career would last from 1948 to 1965, the low level of caps in such a long period of international football is widely believed to be due to his character, which would also see him sent to jail during military service.

139.Jef Mermans   Belgium (6,7)

Belgium vs Netherlands   3-3   13/03/1949 (held for 2 games)

Clubs : Tubantia FAC, Anderlecht, Merksem

International Caps/Goals : - 56/27

Mermans had a prolific goalscoring record at
Anderlecht and not only has a club named for him,
but
the stadium in his native Merksem. Whilst at
Anderlecht he would win seven Belgian titles and
score 367 goals in 399 games. In the international
game, Mermans would represent Belgium in the
1954 World Cup and remains in the top five
goalscorers for the Belgian national team.

141.Trevor Ford   Wales (14)

Wales vs Belgium   1-3   22/05/1949

Clubs : Swansea, Aston Villa, Sunderland, Cardiff
City, PSV, Newport County, Romford

International Caps / Goals : - 38/23

Ford's transfer from Aston Villa to Sunderland at
£30,000 was a world transfer record at the time. He
was later suspended from playing football in Britain
due to illegal payments during his time at
Sunderland.

141.Lucien Pasteur Switzerland (11)

Switzerland vs Wales   4-0   26/05/1949

Clubs : Servette, Urania Geneva, Martigny, Etoile Carouge

International Caps/Goals : 8/3

Pasteur would spend 20 years at Servette from 1936 to 1956 winning three Swiss titles and two Swiss cups during the period.

142.Jean Baratte   France (7)

Francevs Switzerland   4-2   04/06/1949

See Entry 134

143. Agustin Gainza   Spain (5)

Spain vs France   5-1   19/06/1949

Clubs : Athletic Bilbao

International Caps/Goals : 33/10

Gainza was apparently not interested in football and reluctant to enter a career in the sport, doing so at the request of his brother. Gainza would win the Spanish Cup seven times during his career from nine finals.

144. Luis Molowny   Spain (6)

Spain vs Portugal   5-1   02/04/1950

Clubs : Real Madrid, Las Palmas

International Caps/Goals : - 7/2

Molowny would manage Real Madrid on four separate occasions in the 1970s and 1980s winning the UEFA Cup on two occasions and three league titles.. His playing career at Madrid would yield two Spanish league titles and a European Cup

145. Agustin Gainza   Spain (7)

Spain vs Portugal   2-2   09/04/1950

See Entry 143

146.Telmo Zarra   Spain (8,9,10)
Spain vs United States   3-1   25/06/1950 (held
for 3 games)

Clubs : Erandio, Athletic Bilbao, Indautxu, Barakaldo
International Caps : - 20/20

Zarra remains Athletic Bilbao's top scorer in competitive matches and his total of La Liga goals is surpassed only by Messi, however, he remains the top scorer in the history of the Spanish Cup.. The Zarra Trophy given to the top Spanish scorer in La Liga is named for the striker. His three 'Last Goal Wins' Trophies all came in the group stages of the 1950 World Cup.

147.Obdulio Varela Uruguay (1)
Uruguay vs Spain   2-2   09/07/1950

Uruguay's First 'Last Goal Wins' Trophy

Clubs : Montevideo Wanderers, Penarol
International Caps/Goals : - 45/9

Varela captained Uruguay to the 1950 World Cup and is alleged to have attempted to delay the restart following Brazil's goal, in order to settle the crowd. He would win the Uruguayan championship on six occasions with Penarol.

148.Oscar Miguez   Uruguay (2)
Uruguay vs Sweden 3-2   13/07/1950

Clubs : Penarol, Sporting Cristal
International Caps/Goals : - 39/27

Miguez is Uruguay's all time top goalscorer in World Cups having played in the winning side of 1950 and the 1954 tournament, scoring five in the 1950 version and three in the 1954 tournament. He would win six Uruguayan titles at Penarol.

149.Alcides Ghiggia Uruguay (3)

Uruguay vs Brazil   2-1   16/07/1950 **World Cup Final**

Clubs : Sud America, Penarol, Roma, Milan, Danubio

International Caps/Goals : - Uruguay 12/4 Italy 5/1

Ghiggia's winning goal against Brazil in the game known as the '*Maracanazo*' would silence the home crowd and gain a second World Cup for Uruguay. Ghiggia himself noted, 'only three people managed to silence the Maracana: Frank Sinatra, the Pope, and me'[iv] Ghiggia's goal would sneak in at the near post of the Brazilian goalkeeper.

150.Julio Abbadie   Uruguay (4)

Uruguay vs Mexico 3-1   23/03/1952

Clubs : Penarol, Genoa, Lecco
International Caps/Goals : - 26/14

Abbadie scored two goals as part of Uruguay's World Cup squad in 1954. He would spend his career between Italy and Penarol winning the Uruguayan championship on eight occasions and also the Copa Libertadores in 1966.

151.Oscar Miguez   Uruguay (5,6)

Uruguay vs Peru   5-2   30/03/1952 (held for two games)

See Entry 148

152. Francisco Rodrigues   Brazil (2)

Brazil vs Uruguay   4-2   16/04/1952

Clubs : Fluminense, Palmeiras, Botafogo, Juventus, Paulista, Rosario

International Caps / Goals : 21/9

Rodrigues would form part of the 1950 and 1954 Brazil World Cup squads. This goal against Uruguay would cement Brazil's victory in the 1952 Panamerican Championship tournament which would exercise a form of revenge for their shock defeat in the 1950 World Cup.

153.Pinga   Brazil (3)

Brazil vs Chile   3-0   20/04/1952

Clubs : Portuguesa, Vasco da Gama, Juventus
International Caps/Goals : - 17/10

Pinga's formed part of the 1952 Panamerican
Championship winning side and like Rodrigues,
also appeared in the 1950 and 1954 World Cups. He
would score over 400 goals in league football during
his career and be rewarded as a four time player of
the year for Vasco.

154.Victor Ugarte Bolivia (1)
Bolivia vs Brazil   1-8   01/03/1953

Bolivia's First 'Last Goal Wins' Trophy

Clubs : Bolivar, San Lorenzo, Once Caldas
International Caps/Goals : - 45/16

Ugarte remains the second top goalscorer in
Bolivian international football, and is another 'Last
Goal Wins' Trophy winners to have a stadium
named after him, not only in his hometown of
Tupiza, but also in Potosi, Bolivia.

155. Ricardo Alcon Bolivia (2)
Bolivia vs Ecuador   1-1   08/03/1953

Clubs: Union Maestranza de Viacha, Club Litoral,
La Paz

International Caps/goals : 15/3

Alcon's Bolivia career would span from 1953 to 1959[vi] and he would score the equaliser in this Copa America game against Ecuador.

156. Ramon Santos Bolivia (3)

Bolivia   vs Paraguay 1-2   16/03/1953

Clubs : Club Always Ready, Bolivar, La Paz
International Caps/Goals : - 18/3

Ramon Santos was originally born in Argentina but was a naturalised Bolivian.[vii] His late consolation against eventual winners of the Copa America (Paraguay) would not be enough as Bolivia finished second bottom in the tournament.

157. Guillermo Diaz Carmona   Chile (1,2)

Chile vs Bolivia   2-2   28/03/1953 (held for 2 games)

Chile's First 'Last Goal Wins' Trophy

Clubs : Santiago Morning
International Caps 12/3

The game in which Diaz Carmona would score this goal was abandoned due to the behaviour of the Bolivian players resulting in a six month ban for one Bolivian, for kicking the referee. In a match against Santiago Wanderers in 1952, Guillermo Diaz would score for Santiago Morning, whilst another Guillermo Diaz (Zambrona) would score for the opponents. The two Guillermo Diazs would have concurrent careers, with Carmona gaining more caps for the national team.[viii]

158. George Robledo Chile (3)
Chile vs Peru 2-1   26/07/1953

Clubs : Barnsley, Newcastle, Colo Colo, Deportivo O'Higgins
International Caps / Goals : - 31/8

Robledo had an English mother, and grew up in South Yorkshire. He was the first South American to appear in an FA Cup final (along with his brother Ted), and also scored the most goals in a season in the English top flight for a player not from Britain or Ireland until the 1990s.

159. Cornelio Heredia   Peru (1)
Peru vs Chile 5-0   28/07/1953

Peru's First 'Last Goal Wins' Trophy

Clubs :- Alfonso Ugarte de Puno, Alianza Lima, Ciclista Lima

International Caps / Goals : - 24/2

Cornelio Heredia would win four Peruvian titles for Alianza Lima, and was known by the nickname of 'El Brujo' or the wizard. Heredia would only begin his career at the age of 26, before moving to Alianza in 1948 at the age of 28.

160. Braulio Musso Chile (4)

Chile vs Peru 2-1   17/09/1954

Clubs : Universidad de Chile

International Caps/ Goals : - 14/3

Musso would be part of Chile's third place squad in their home World Cup, but would not appear in any of the fixtures. He would win five Chilean titles at Universidad de Chile in his seventeen year career at the club.

161. Oscar Gomez Sanchez   Peru (2)

Peru vs Chile 4-2   19/09/1954

Clubs: Alianza Lima, River Plate, Gimnasia y Esgrima La Plata

International Caps/Goals : - 26/14

Sanchez formed part of the Peru teams at the 1953, 1955, 1956 and 1959 Copa America tournaments, finishing third on two occasions and fourth at the final one. He would win three Peruvian league titles with Alianza Lima

162. Jaime Ramirez Chile (5)

Chile vs Peru 5-4   06/03/1955

Clubs : Universidad de Chile, Espanyol, Colo Colo, Granada, CD O'Higgins, Racing Club, Audax Italiano, Huachipato Talcahuano, Palestino, Union San Felipe

International Caps/Goals : - 43/10

Part of Chile's 1962 and 1966 World Cup squads, Ramirez would represent clubs in Chile, Argentina and Spain in his twenty two year career. His management career would see him take in another country by managing Olimpia de Honduras.

163. Enrique Hormazabal   Chile (6)

Chile vs Uruguay   2-2   13/03/1955

Clubs : Santiago Morning, Colo Colo

International Caps/Goals : - 47/17

Hormazabal received two runners up medals in the Copa America for Chile, and also secured three Chilean titles with Colo Colo. Hormazabal would be top scorer at the 1956 Copa America, and is still considered one of the greatest Chilean players of all time.

164. Manuel Munoz   Chile (7)

Chile vs Paraguay   5-0   20/03/1955

Clubs : Colo Colo, Fernandez Vial Concepcion, Audax Italiano

International Caps/Goals : - 27/8

Munoz would also form part of the Colo Colo championship winning sides and represented Chile in the 1950 World Cup and consecutive runners up finishes in the Copa America tournaments of 1955 and 1956.

165. Rodolfo Micheli   Argentina (1)

Argentina vs Chile   1-0   30/05/1955

Argentina's First 'Last Goal Wins' Trophy

Clubs : Argentino de Quilmes, Independiente, River Plate, Huracan, Millonarios, Platense

International Caps/Goals : - 13/10

Eight of Micheli's ten international goals were scored in the 1955 Copa America, where he finished as top scorer and would assist Argentina's victory in the tournament, Micheli spent one season in Colombia with Milonarios with the remainder of his career in his native Argentina.

166. Roberto Drago   Peru (3)

Peru vs Argentina   1-2   22/01/1956

Clubs : Deportivo Arica, Centro Iqueno, Deportivo Muncipal, Racing Club, Independiente Medellin

International Caps/Goals : - 30/9

Drago's three sons would follow him into football – all playing for Deportivo Municipal.[ix]His grandson, Ignacio Drago is a current professional footballer also, whilst his brother played basketball for the Peruvian national team. He would be part of the Deportivo Municipal side which won three Peruvian titles in 1940, 1943 and 1950.

167. Oscar Miguez   Uruguay (7)

Uruguay vs Peru   2-0   28/01/1956

See Entry 148

168. Jaime Ramirez   Chile (8)

Chile vs Uruguay   1-2   06/02/1956

See Entry 162

169.Oscar Gomez Sanchez   Peru (4,5)

Peru vs Chile 3-4   09/02/1956 (held for 2 games)

See Entry 161

170.Larry De Faria   Brazil (4)

Brazil vs Peru   1-0   06/03/1956

Clubs : Fluminense, Internacional
International Caps/Goals : - 6/4

Larry Pinto de Faria won Olympic Gold for Brazil at
the 1952 games, where he would be the top scorer
with four goals, and also the 1956 Panamerican
championship. He would later become a sports
commentator on local Brazilian TV.

171.Bodinho   Brazil (5)

Brazil vs Mexico   2-1   08/03/1956

Clubs : Ibis, Sampaio Correa, Flamengo, Nacional, Internacional

Bodinho and De Faria (**Entry 170)** would form a deadly strike partnership at Internacional scoring over 400 goals between them in their respective times at the club. He would win the Campeaonato Gaucho (the regional Brazilian football league for the state of Rio Grande Do Sul) on five occasions.

172.Chinesinho   Brazil (6)

Brazil vs Costa Rica 7-1   13/03/1956

Clubs : Renner, Internacional, Palmeiras, Modena, Catania, Juventus, Lanerossi Vicenza, New York Cosmos, Nacional-SP
International Caps / Goals : - 17/7

Born Sidney Colonia Cunha, his nickname translates as 'little Chinese'. Chinesinho would form part of the 1956 Panamerican Championship winning squad and the 1959 Copa American runners up, but would miss out on the 1958 World Cup win.

173.Omar Sivori   Argentina (2)

Argentina vs Brazil 2-2   18/03/1956

Clubs : River Plate, Juventus, Napoli

International Caps/Goals : - Argentina 19/9 Italy 9/8

Sivori won both the Copa America and the European Footballer of the Year award, however, his move to Juventus would see him banned from the Argentinian national side and represent Italy in the 1962 World Cup.[x] Sivori's partnership with the Welshman, John Charles, would lead Juventus to several titles and cups in Italy. He still holds the record for the most goals scored in a single Serie A match, with six in a 9-1 victory over Inter Milan

174.Ernesto Grillo   Argentina (3,4)

Argentina vs Uruguay   2-1   01/07/1956 (held for 2 games)

Clubs : Independiente, AC Milan, Boca Juniors

International Caps/Goals : - 21/8

Ernesto Grillo is enrolled in the Argentinian football hall of fame, notably for scoring a goal in a 3-1 defeat of England in 1953. Grillo would win Serie A with Milan before returning to Argentina to win three league titles with Boca Juniors in the 1960s.

175.Norberto Conde   Argentina
(5)

Argentina vs Paraguay   1-0   15/08/1956

Clubs : Velez Sarsfield, Huracan, Atlanta, Ferro, America de Cali

International Caps/Goals : - 12/3

Conde would make sporadic appearances for Argentina in the three years from 1955-1958 including as part of the Copa America winning side of 1955. In 1954, Conde was the top scorer in the Argentinian top division

176.Antonio Valentin Angellillo   Argentina
(6)

Argentina vs Czechoslovakia   1-0   19/08/1956

Clubs : Racing, Boca Juniors, Internazionale, Roma, AC Milan, Lecco, Genoa

International Caps/Goals : Argentina 11/11 Italy 2/1

Angellillo like Sivori **(Entry 173)** was banned from the Argentine national team for signing for an Italian club. He shares the record for most goals in a season at Inter Milan with Giuseppe Meazza **(Entry 90)** and like Meazza would represent both Milan sides. He would win his sole Serie A title at AC Milan in 1968.

177.Antonio Garabal   Argentina (7,8)

Argentina vs Uruguay   2-2   14/11/1956
(held for two games, no further appearances for Argentina)

Clubs : Ferro, Atletico Madrid, Boca Juniors, San Lorenzo
International Caps/Goals : 3 / 4

Garabal would reluctantly sign for Atletico Madrid from his hometown club of Ferro, which would effectively end his international career, recognising the potential financial benefits such a move would have on him. He would return to Ferro to also work as a coach.[xi]

178.Humberto Maschio   Argentina (9)

Argentina vs Colombia   8-2   13/03/1957

Clubs : Quilmes, Racing Club, Bologna, Atalanta, Internazionale, Fiorentina, Racing Club

International Caps / Goals : - Argentina 18/18 Italy 4/0

The final of the 'Angels with Dirty Faces' trio with Sivori and Angellilo, Maschio captained Italy at the 1962 World Cup following his Argentina ban. He would have his nose broken by Leonel Sanchez in the 'Battle of Santiago' during this World Cup. His time at Inter would yield a solitary Serie A title.

179.Antonio Valentin Angellillo (10)   Argentina

Argentina vs Ecuador   3-0   17/03/1957

See Entry 176

180.Jose Sanfillipo (11)   Argentina

Argentina vs Uruguay   4-0   20/03/1957

Clubs : San Lorenzo, Boca Juniors, Nacional, Banfield, Bangu, Bahia, San Miguel

International Caps/Goals : 29/21

Sanfillipo's time at Boca would be shortlived, ending due to a serious bout of indiscipline in punching an opponent.[xii] When he was not smacking his opponents, Sanfilipo was a prolific goalscorer, finishing as top scorer in the Argentinian top flight on four occasions and being the top scorer in the 1959 Copa America tournament.

181.Omar Corbatta   Argentina (12)

Argentina vs Chile 6-2   28/03/1957

Clubs : Racing Club, Boca Juniors, Independiente Medellin, San Telmo, Italia Unidos, Tiro Federal

International Caps/Goals : - 43/18

Corbatta struggled with drink problems throughout his career, even being drunk on the field of play. Furthermore, he never learned to read. A bronze statue of Corbatta stands in the Racing Club hall of fame. Corbatta would win the Copa America twice with Argentina in 1957 and 1959 and also appear in the 1958 World Cup in Sweden.

182.Osvaldo Cruz   Argentina (13)

Argentina vs Brazil 3-0   03/04/1957

Clubs: Independiente, Palmerias, Union Espanola

International Caps/Goals : - 21/3

Cruz would win the Brazilian Cup whilst at Palmeiras and the Argentine Championship at Independiente. He would represent Argentina at the 1958 World Cup bookended by two Copa America titles.

183.Alberto Terry   Peru (6)

Peru vs Argentina   2-1   06/04/1957

Clubs : Universitario, Sporting Cristal
International Caps/Goals: - 25/11

Terry would be an important player in the history of Peruvian football as well as that of Univeritario, winning the Peruvian league title at his first club in 1949 and following this up with victory for Sporting Cristal, twelve years later in 1961.

184.Indio   Brazil (7)

Brazil vs Peru   1-1   13/04/1957

Clubs : Flamengo, Corinthians, Espanyol, Lusitano Evora, Sanjoanense, America FC

International Caps/Goals : - 7/2

Indio is the last surviving member of Brazil's 1954 World Cup quarter finalist squad. He would win three state championships in his time at Flamengo. Indio would score three goals in the largest victory for Flamengo in the Maracana, a 12-2 thrashing of Sao Cristovao in 1956.

185.Didi   Brazil (8)

Brazil vs Peru   1-0   21/04/1957

Clubs : Madureira, Fluminense, Botafogo, Real Madrid, Sporting Cristal, CD Veracruz, Sao Paulo

International Caps/ Goals : - 68/20

Didi is widely considered as the inventor of the *folha seca* free kick technique whereby the ball dips unexpectedly. He would win the World Cup twice with Brazil in three tournaments, picking up the golden ball for best player in the 1958 tournament. It is widely believed that Didi scored the first goal at the Maracana Stadium and is attributed with the phrase *jogo bonito*, the beautiful game.

186.Tite   Brazil (9)

Brazil vs Portugal   2-1   11/06/1957

Clubs : Goytacaz, Fluminense, Santos, Corinthians

International Caps/Goals : 3/1

Augusto Vieira de Oliviera also known as Tite, would only score one international goal on his debut against Portugal. He would play alongside Pele at Santos and win two titles at the club in his two spells at the Sao Paulo club.

187.Del Vecchio   Brazil (10)

Brazil vs Portugal   3-0   16/06/1957

Clubs : Santos, Verona, Napoli, Padova, Milan, Boca Juniors, Sao Paulo, Bangu, Atletico Paranense

International Caps/Goals : - 9/1

Del Vecchio was of Italian origin and would spend a large amount of his career in Italy, winning Serie A with Milan in 1962. His international career would involve a fourth place finish at the 1956 South American Championships. Del Vecchio would make way for Pele when the latter made his debut for the Brazilian national team in the side's next fixture.

188.Miguel Juarez   Argentina (14)

Argentina vs Brazil 2-1   07/07/1957

Clubs : Belgrano, Rosario Central, Union Sante Fe, Central Cordoba

International Caps/Goals : - 5/2

Juarez is another who would be part of Argentina's 1957 Copa America triumph. This game would be notable as the first appearance of Pele, and his first international goal for Brazil. Juarez would give Cesar Luis Menotti his first coaching job at Newell's Old Boys, before Menotti would later go on to manage Argentina to the 1978 World Cup.

189.Mazzola   Brazil (11)

Brazil vs Argentina 2-0   10/07/1957

Clubs : Palmeiras, Milan, Napoli, Juventus, Chiasso, Mendrisiostar
International Caps/Goals : - Brazil 8/4 Italy 6/5

Mazzola was born Jose Altafini, and was named for Italian footballer Valentin Mazzola. He is credited with creating the saying 'golazo' in Italian football and is a notable commentator in Italy. His career in Italy would see him win two Serie A titles each with Milan and Juventus and finish as top scorer in the competition in 1962.

190.Joel   Brazil (12)

Brazil vs Bulgaria   4-0   14/05/1958

Clubs : Botafogo, Flamengo, Valencia, Vitoria
International Caps/Goals : - 14/3

Joel would start the first two matches of the 1958 World Cup before making way with his teammate, Dida for Garrincha and Pele. Joel would win the Rio State Championship with Flamengo on three occassions.

191.Mazzola   Brazil (13,14)

Brazil vs Austria   3-0   08/06/1958 (held for 2 games)

See Entry 189

192.Pele   Brazil (15)

Brazil vs Wales   1-0   19/06/1958

Clubs : Santos, New York Cosmos
International Caps/Goals : - 92/77

Perhaps the most famous player in the history of football, Pele would score a 'thousand' goals in his career, win three World Cups, two Copa Libertadores, ten Brazilian championships and countless other individual awards. Pele's greatest moment would come in the Second World War, where he would score an overhead kick to equalise for the Allies against Nazi Germany, which led the way from their escape from the stadium. This goal, in the quarter final of the World Cup would be a sharp turn and stabbed finished from within the box, sealing victory and a semi final place for Brazil.

193.Roger Piantoni France (8)

France vs Brazil   2-5   24/06/1958

Clubs : Nancy, Reims, Nice

International Caps/Goals : - 37/18

Piantoni's late consolation against Brazil would be his last goal in the tournament, needing emergency surgery for appendicitis prior to the third/fourth place playoff against West Germany. Whilst at Reims, Piantoni would win three Ligue 1 titles and a Coupe de France.

194.Uwe Seeler   West Germany (1)

West Germany vs France   2-2   26/10/1958

West Germany's First 'Last Goal Wins' Trophy

Clubs : Hamburger SV, Cork City

International Caps/Goals : - 72/43

Seeler had a long and illustrious career, appearing in four World Cups, although his appearances are bookended by German wins in 1954 and 1974. He was the first player to appear in 20 World Cup Games, the first player to score in four World Cups and the first player to score at least two goals in four World Cups.

195.Helmut Rahn   West Germany (2)

West Germany vs Austria   2-2   19/11/1958

Clubs: Rot-Weiss Essen, FC Koln, SC Enschede, Meidericher SV

International Caps/Goals : - 40/21

Rahn was runner up in the Ballon d'or in 1958 following a silver boot award at the World Cup. His exploits in the 1954 World Cup final, scoring two (including the winner) and assisting the other in the 3-2 victory over Hungary gives him legendary status in German football.

196.Uwe Seeler   West Germany (3)

West Germany vs Bulgaria 3-0   21/12/1958

See Entry 194

197.Erich Juskowiak   West Germany (4)

West Germany vs Scotland 2-3   06/05/1959

Clubs : RW Oberhausen, SSV 04 Wuppertal, Fortuna Dusseldorf

International Caps/Goals : - 31/4

Juskowiak would make his debut for West Germany in 1951 but not make another appearance until after the World Cup win of 1954. He became the first German player to be sent off in a World Cup in 1958 during the semi final with Sweden.

198.Erwin Stein   West Germany (5)

West Germany vs Poland 1-1   20/05/1959 (no further appearances for West Germany)

Clubs : Eintrach Frankfurt, SV Darmstadt, SpVgg Griesheim 02

International Caps/Goals : - 1/1

Stein's only international appearance yielded his only goal, playing for West Germany despite being an amateur. His signature for Eintracht Frankfurt, where he would score two goals in a European Cup final, made him ineligible for the 1960 Olympics, which allegedly caused a rift with the then national manager.

199.Erich Juskowiak   West Germany (6)

West Germany vs Switzerland   4-0   04/10/1959

See Entry 197

200.Gerhard Siedl   West Germany (7)

West Germany vs Netherlands   7-0   21/10/1959

Clubs : Bayern Munich, Borussia Neunkirchen, 1. FC Saarbrucken, Karlruher SC, FC Basel, AZ, Austria Salzburg

International Caps / Goals : - Saarland 16/4 West Germany 6/3

Siedl would start his international career playing for Saarland, which was part of the French Occupation zone following the Second World War. After the dissolution of the Saar as a separate entity to West Germany, Saar players were able to represent the Federal Republic. Siedl would win two German cups in the late fifties whilst at Karlsruhe and Bayern Munich.

201.Albert Brulls   West Germany (8)

West Germany vs Hungary   3-4   08/11/1959

Clubs : Borussia Monchengladbach, FC Modena, Brescia Calcio, BSC Young Boys, VfR Neuss

International Caps / Goals : - 25/9

Brulls would represent West Germany in both the 1962 and 1966 World Cups, having already became one of the first German footballers to play abroad by representing Modena. Brulls would win the German Cup during his time at Monchengladbach.

202.Alfred Schmidt   West Germany (9)

West Germany vs Yugoslavia   1-1
          20/12/1959

Clubs : Borussia Dortmund

International Caps/ Goals : - 25/8

Schmidt would spend his entire professional career at Dortmund, winning the German championship twice and adding a German Cup and European Cup Winners Cup to those titles. His international career would see him represent West Germany in the 1958 World Cup, where they would secure a fourth place finish.

1960 – 1974
Escape to Victory

Between 1960 and 1974, the 'Last Goal Wins' Trophy would spend much of it's time in Europe, with Peru, Chile and Brazil being the only non-European nations to hold the trophy. Finland would gain it's first title, as the trophy passed through familiar faces and returning for a consolidated spell amongst the Home Nations. Scotland's failure to qualify for both the 1966 and 1970 editions of the World Cup would mean that the title would not be contested during the tournament, with Gerson's absence from the Brazil squad in 1962 meaning that this World Cup would also not see the trophy.

Countries

West Germany
Portugal
Yugoslavia
England
Spain
Peru
Chile
Brazil
Switzerland
Italy
Finland
Scotland

Northern Ireland
Belgium
Netherlands
Czechoslovakia
Poland
Wales

Players

203.Uwe Seeler　　West Germany (10)

West Germany vs Chile　　2-1　　23/03/1960

See Entry 194

204.Cavem　　Portugal (1)

Portugal vs West Germany 1-2　　27/04/1960

Portugal's First 'Last Goal Wins' Trophy

Clubs : Lusitano, Covilha, Benfica

International Caps / Goals : - 18/5

Cavem would win Portugal's first 'Last Goal Wins'
Trophy, and represent Benfica in 4 European Cup
Finals and win two of them in 1961 and 1962.
Benfica's dominance in Portuguese football in the
1960s would see him win nine titles.

205.Borivoje Kostic   Yugoslavia (4)

Yugoslavia vs Portugal   1-2   08/05/1960

Clubs : Red Star Belgrade, Vicenza, St Louis
International Caps / Goals : - 33/26

A prolific goal scorer who remains Red Star's all
time top scorer, Kostic would end his career in the
North American Soccer League. Kostic would form
part of the Yugoslavia squad who finished as
runners up to the USSR in the 1960 European
Championships.

206.Johnny Haynes England (36)

England vs Yugoslavia   3-3   11/05/1960

Clubs : Fulham, Wimbledon, Toronto, Durban City,
Wealdstone

International Caps / Goals : - 56/18

Haynes would represent Fulham for 18 years and became the first player to earn £100 a week, following the removal of the maximum wage in English football in 1961. His international career would effectively be ended by a car crash in 1962, never being picked for the national side following the incident which saw him break his feet and be out of action for a year. A statue of Haynes stands outside Craven Cottage.

207.Eulogio Martinez   Spain (11)

Spain vs England   3-0   15/05/1960

Clubs : Libertad, Barcelona, Elche, Atletico Madrid, Europa

International Caps / Goals : - Paraguay 9/4 Spain 8/6

Born in Paraguay, Martinez would become known for the 'Martinez turn' later popularised as the 'Cruyff turn'. His career would see him win two Spanish titles with Barcelona during a time when Real Madrid dominated the European Cup.

208.Jose Carrasco   Peru (7)

Peru vs Spain   1-3   10/07/1960

Clubs : Deportivo Muncipal

International Caps/Goals 9/2

Carrasco was part of the Peru side which beat England 4-1 in 1959, bizarrely being given a rating of 5/10 in the next days' newspaper, and also part of that year's Copa America squad which would see Peru finish fourth.

209.Leonel Sanchez   Chile (9)

Chile vs Peru 5-2   19/03/1961

Clubs : Universidad de Chile, Colo Colo, Palestino, Ferroviarios
International Caps/Goals : - 85/24

Sanchez played a major role in the 'Battle of Santiago' fixture in the 1962 World Cup, punching two Italian players and breaking Humberto Maschio's (**Entry 178**) nose. [xiii]He would also win the Golden Boot and be named in the All Star team of Chile's home World Cup. He would win six Chilean league titles with Universidad, adding a final title in 1970 with Colo Colo.

210.Eladio Rojas   Chile (10)

Chile vs West Germany   3-1   26/03/1961

Clubs : Everton (Chile) River Plate, Colo Colo

International Caps/Goals: 25/3

Rojas goal in the 90th minute of the third/fourth place play off against Yugoslavia in the 1962 World Cup would secure third place for Chile. Picking up the ball just inside the opposition half, Rojas would hit a low shot which wrong footed the Yugoslav keeper via a divot in the pitch.

211.Juan Soto   Chile (11)

Chile vs Brazil   1-2   07/05/1961

Clubs : Colo Colo, Rangers de Talca, Audaz Italiano, San Antonio Unido
International Caps / Goals : - 22/7

Juan Soto-Mura was nicknamed 'Nino-Gol' for his boyish looks whilst at Colo Colo, where he would win the Chilean title and cup. His time at Colo Colo would see him top scorer for four consecutive seasons upon arrival at the club in 1957.

212.Gerson   Brazil (16)

Brazil vs Chile   1-0   11/05/1961

Clubs : Flamengo, Botafogo, Sao Paulo, Fluminense
International Caps/Goals : - 70/14

Gerson would form part of the 1970 Brazil World Cup winning squad, also making the All-Star team and scoring in the final. Gerson would be known after football for starring in a cigarette advert which became synonymous with corruption due to the tagline, *'You too take advantage'*. Domestically, he would win the Rio and Sao Paulo State Championship on three occasions each

213.Pepe   Brazil (17)

Brazil vs Argentina 2-3   13/04/1963

Clubs : Santos
International Caps/Goals : - 41/22

Pele's foil throughout his time at Santos, Pepe would score over 400 goals for the club. At international level, Pepe would be part of the Brazil squads which won the World Cups in 1958 and 1962 but not play in either tournament. Pepe would remark that he was the best player in the world, because Pele 'didn't count as he was from Saturn'.[xiv]

214.Amarildo   Brazil (18)

Brazil vs Argentina 5-2   16/04/1963

Clubs : Flamengo, Botafogo, Milan, Fiorentina, Roma, Vasco da Gama

International Caps/Goals : 20/7

Amarildo scored three goals in the 1962 World Cup, replacing Pele in the tournament. His managerial career was perhaps less successful, lasting one week in charge of America (Brazil) in 2008.[xv]

215.Jose Augusto de Almeida   Portugal (2)

Portugal vs Brazil   1-0   21/04/1963

Clubs : Barreirense, Benfica
International Caps / Goals : - 45/9

Jose Augusto's first international goal would come in this game, halfway through his international career. He would go on to manage Portugal in the early 1970s and the Portugal Women's team in the mid 2000s.

216.Norbert Eschmann   Switzerland (12)

Switzerland vs Portugal   2-3   29/04/1963

Clubs : Lausanne Sports, Red Star, Servette, Marseille, Stade Francais, Lausanne Sports, Sion, Young Boys, Locarno, Martigny

International Caps / Goals : - 15/3

Born in France, Eschmann would represent Switzerland in his international career and play for the Alpine nation in both the 1954 and 1962 World Cups. Upon retirement, he would become a journalist for the daily newspaper '24 heures'.

217.Gianni Rivera   Italy (9)

Italy vs Switzerland 3-1   10/05/1964

Clubs : Alessandria, Milan

International Caps/Goals : - 60/14

Rivera would take part in four World Cups, win three Serie A titles and two European Cups whilst at Milan, scoring the winning goal against West Germany in a seven goal thriller, to take Italy to the World Cup final in 1970. In 1969, Rivera would win the Ballon d'or, judged the best player in Europe. He is currently a sitting member of the European Parliament and has taken part in the Italian version of Strictly Come Dancing.

218.Juhani Peltonen   Finland (1)

Finland vs   Italy   1-6   04/11/1964

Finland's First 'Last Goal Wins' Trophy

Clubs : Valkeakosken Haka, Hamburg

International Caps / Goals : - 68/11

Peltonen was a three time Finnish footballer of the year, and the first Finn to play in Germany. His time at Hamburg would end due to a contractual dispute, returning to Finland to play for Haka again.

219. John Greig   Scotland (31)

Scotland vs Finland 2-1   27/05/1965

Clubs : Glasgow Rangers

International Caps/Goals : - 44/3

Greig spent all of his career at Rangers, and was named the greatest ever player for the side[xvi]. During their victorious Cup Winners Cup campaign in 1972, Greig stated that he would not look to shave until Rangers had won the competition.[xvii]

220. Willie Irvine   Northern Ireland (1)

Northern Ireland vs Scotland   3-2   02/10/1965

Northern Ireland's First 'Last Goal Wins' Trophy

Clubs : Burnley, Preston, Brighton, Halifax Town, Great Harwood

International Caps/Goals : - 23/8

Irvine's career would peter out following a serious broken leg at Burnley in 1968, although his career would continue for a further six years, he never hit the same levels and finished his career in the Northern Premier League (which is currently the seventh tier of the English football pyramid).

221. Alan Peacock   England (37)

England vs Northern Ireland   2-1   10/11/1965
(no further appearances for England)

Clubs: - Middlesbrough, Leeds, Plymouth Argyle
International Caps / Goals : - 6/3

Peacock's last international appearance for England after he had represented them in the 1962 World Cup, would see him gain the 'Last Goal Wins' Trophy. Injuries blighted his career following this point and he eventually became a newsagent.

222. Roger Hunt   England (38)

England vs Spain   2-0   08/12/1965

Clubs : Liverpool, Bolton Wanderers, Hellenic
International Caps/Goals : - 34/18

Hunt formed part of the England World Cup winning squad in 1966, playing in every game and scoring three goals in the process. Hunt would be Liverpool's top scorer for 23 years, until overtaken by Ian Rush, and his time at Liverpool would see the Merseyside club lift two top division titles.

223. Bobby Moore   England (39)
England vs Poland   1-1   05/01/1966

Clubs : West Ham United, Fulham, San Antonio Thunder, Seattle Sounders, Herning Fremad, Carolina Lightnin'
International Caps/Goals : - 108/2

One of two international goals for Bobby Moore, Moore would captain England to their home World Cup victory in 1966, and is commemorated by a statue at Wembley stadium. His tackle on Jairzinho in the 1970 World Cup is fondly remembered and referred to in the song – 'Three Lions'. A local Essex lad, Moore's time with West Ham would be one of the most successful in their history winning the European Cup Winners' Cup. Along with Pele, Moore also represented the Allies in the Second World War against Nazi Germany.

224. Nobby Stiles   England (40)
England vs West Germany 1-0   23/02/1966

Clubs : Manchester United, Middlesbrough, Preston North End
International Caps/ Goals : - 28/1

Stiles only goal in an England shirt, he would also form part of the World Cup winning squad, where his dancing celebration would become a memorable element of the victory. Stiles wore false teeth and thick glasses outside of the game making him an unlikely looking footballer. His time in the Manchester United side saw him win the European Cup and the English title twice, acting as a defensive counterbalance to Bobby Charlton, George Best and Denis Law.

225. Jimmy Johnstone   Scotland (32)
Scotland vs England   3-4   02/04/1966

Clubs: Celtic, San Jose Earthquakes, Sheffield United, Dundee, Shelbourne, Elgin City
International Caps/Goals : 23/4

Johnstone played a key part in the 'Lisbon Lions' Celtic European Cup winning side, along with 9 consecutive championships for the club in Sixties and Seventies. Named the club's best player in 2002[xviii], Johnstone would die at the age of 61 from Motor Neurone Disease.

226. Denis Law   Scotland (33)
Scotland vs Wales   1-1   22/10/1966

Clubs : Huddersfield Town, Manchester City, Torino, Manchester United
International Caps/Goals : - 55/30

Law would successively be involved in three British record transfers from Huddersfield to Manchester City to Torino and then onto Manchester United and also win the Ballon d'Or in 1964. Along with being the joint top scorer for Scotland, he remains the third highest scorer in Manchester United colours behind Wayne Rooney and Bobby Charlton and a statue of Law stands outside Old Trafford. It is widely believed that Law's goal for Manchester City against Manchester United in the 1973/74 season relegated his former club, however, they would have been relegated regardless of the defeat.

227. Geoff Hurst   England (41)
England vs Scotland   2-3   15/04/1967

Clubs: West Ham United, Stoke City, Cape Town City, West Bromwich Albion, Cork Celtic, Seattle Sounders
International Caps/ Goals : - 49/24

Hurst's consolation goal in the game which Scottish fans jokingly suggested made them Unofficial World Champions came following his exploits in winning the World Cup where he would become the first (and so far) only player to score a hat trick in a World Cup final. He also played first class cricket for Essex.

228. Roger Hunt   England (42)
England vs Spain   2-0   24/05/1967

See Entry 222

229. Alan Ball   England (43,44)
England vs Austria 1-0   27/05/1967 (held for 2 games)

Clubs : Ashton United, Blackpool, Everton, Arsenal, Hellenic, Southampton, Philadelphia Fury, Vancouver Whitecaps, Floreat Athena, Eastern AA, Bristol Rovers
International Caps/Goals: 72/8

Ball, another member of England's World Cup winning squad would be subject to a British record transfer in 1971 as he moved from Everton to Arsenal. As a manager, Ball would preside over Man City's relegation from the Premier League in 1996, telling the City players to hold onto the ball and keep a draw in their final game, incorrectly believing this would be sufficient to maintain their top flight status.

230. Martin Peters   England (45)
England vs Soviet Union   2-2   06/12/1967

Clubs : West Ham United, Tottenham Hotspur, Norwich City, Sheffield United
International Caps/ Goals : - 67/20

Another World Cup winner, Peters scored to give England the lead in the 1966 final. Also part of the West Ham side which would win the European Cup Winners Cup, Peters would add to that title with a UEFA Cup whilst at Tottenham.

231.John Hughes   Scotland (34)
Scotland vs England   1-1   24/02/1968

Clubs : Celtic, Crystal Palace, Sunderland
International Caps/Goals : - 8/1

Hughes' only international goal would come in a draw in the British Home Championships of 1967/68. He missed Celtic's European triumph in Lisbon due to injury but did feature in enough appearances in the tournament to secure a winners' medal.

232. Billy Bremner Scotland (35)
Scotland vs Austria 2-1   06/11/1968

Clubs : Leeds United, Hull City, Doncaster Rovers
International Caps/Goals :- 54/3

Bremner was a combative midfielder who would captain Leeds United in their most successful period winning the English title on two occasions and the FA Cup. A statue of him sits outside Leeds United's home ground, Elland Road.

233. Colin Stein   Scotland (36)
Scotland vs Cyprus 5-0   11/12/1968

Clubs : Hibernian, Rangers, Coventry City, Kilmarnock
International Caps/ Goals : - 21/9

Stein would score four goals in the return fixture of this World Cup qualifier against Cyprus, another Scottish player wouldn't score a hat trick in international football until 2015. Stein's equaliser against Celtic for Rangers in 1971 would be overshadowed by the second Ibrox disaster occurring moments later, caused by a collapsed barrier on a stairway and leading to the deaths of 66 people.

234. Tommy McLean   Scotland (37)
Scotland vs Wales   5-3   03/05/1969

Clubs : Kilmarnock, Rangers
International Caps/Goals : - 6/1

McLean's short international career was somewhat in contrast to his storied domestic career which would lead four Scottish titles, three with Rangers and one with Kilmarnock.

235. John O'Hare   Scotland (38)
Scotland vs Northern Ireland   1-0   18/04/1970
(held for 4 games)

Clubs : Sunderland, Vancouver Royal Canadians, Derby County, Leeds United, Nottingham Forest, Dallas Tornado
International Caps / Goals : - 13/5

O'Hare would hold onto the title for four games including two goalless draws sandwiched between single goal victories against Northern Ireland and Denmark. O'Hare would follow Brian Clough throughout much of his career, winning titles at Derby and Nottingham Forest and two European Cups with Forest

236. Paul van Himst   Belgium (8)
Belgium vs Scotland   3-0   03/02/1971

Clubs : Anderlecht, Molenbeek, Eendracht Aalst
International Caps/Goals : - 81/30

van Himst would represent Belgium as a player and a manager in the 1970 and 1994 World Cups respectively. Van Himst is another player who would play for the Allies against Nazi Germany in the Second World War.

237. Andre de Nul   Belgium (9)

Belgium vs Portugal   3-0   17/02/1971

Clubs : Eendracht Aalst, Lierse, Anderlecht, Union SG, Rot-Weiss Essen
International Caps/Goals : - 3/2

De Nul's final international cap would come in his next appearance against Luxembourg. In his career, he would win the Belgian cup twice, with Lierse and Anderlecht and a sole Belgian title in 1974.

238. Wilfried van Moer   Belgium (10)

Belgium vs Luxembourg   4-0   20/05/1971

Clubs : Beveren, Antwerp, Standard Liege, Beringen, Sint Truiden

International Caps/Goals : - 57/9

Van Moer would play for Belgium in the 1970 and 1982 World Cups, appearing in the later tournament at the age of 37. He would manage the Belgian national side for 5 games in 1996 before being dismissed.

239. Erwin Vandendaele   Belgium (11)

Belgium vs Luxembourg   1-0   07/11/1971

Clubs : Club Brugge, Anderlecht, Stade de Reims, Gent
International Caps/Goals : - 32/1

Vandendaele, although born in Metz, France, would represent the Belgian national side throughout the 1970s. This would be his only international goal. Whilst at Anderlecht, he would win the European Cup Winners Cup and finish as runners up in the same competition the following year.

240. John O'Hare   Scotland (39)

Scotland vs Belgium   1-0   10/11/1971

See Entry 235

241. Barry Hulshoff   Netherlands (5)

Netherlands vs Scotland   2-1   01/12/1971

Clubs : Ajax, Grazer AK

International Caps/Goals : - 12/6

Hulshoff formed part of the Ajax side which won three consecutive European Cups in the 1970s. He would make a cameo appearance in the Dutch film, 'Op de Hollandse Toer'. His post-playing career would see him largely managing in Belgium taking in such sides as Lierse and Beerschot.

242. Johan Cruyff   Netherlands (6)

Netherlands vs Greece   5-0   16/02/1972

Clubs : Ajax, Barcelona, Los Angeles Aztecs, Washington Diplomats, Levante, Feyenoord

International Caps/Goals : - 48/33

Cruyff is remembered as the finest Dutch footballer of not only his generation but also in history. Cruyff would win the European Cup three times with Ajax and reach a World Cup final with the Netherlands. In the same World Cup his feint and turn against Sweden became known as the 'Cruyff Turn'. Cruyff has had a strong influence on the tactical development of the game, being part of the Total Football at Ajax and laying the foundations of 'tiki-taka' in Spain with Barcelona.

243. Dirk Schneider   Netherlands (7)

Netherlands vs Peru   3-0   03/05/1972

Clubs : Go Ahead Eagles, Feyenoord, Vitesse Arnhem, FC Wageningen.
International Caps/Goals : - 11/2

Schneider would win two titles and a UEFA cup whilst at Feyenoord, with the first coming in 1971 despite the dominance of the Ajax side in Europe that year. He would miss out on a place at the 1974 World Cup.

244. Vladimir Hagara   Czechoslovakia (3)

Czechoslovakia vs Netherlands   1-2   30/08/1972

Clubs : TJ Gottwaldov, Nitra, Spartak Trnava,
Strojarne Martin, Slovan Piestany
International Caps/Goals : 25/4

Born in the western Slovak region of Trnava,
Hagara would be part of the Czechoslovak 1970
World Cup squad eliminated in the group stage by
eventual winners Brazil and holders England.
Spartak Trnava would dominate Czechoslovak
football at the turn of the decade with Hagara in the
side, winning the Czechoslovak title five times
between 1968 and 1973.

245. Robert Gadocha   Poland (1)

Poland   vs Czechoslovakia 3-0   15/10/1972

Poland's First 'Last Goal Wins' Trophy

Clubs : Wawel Krakow, Legia Warsaw, Nantes,
Chicago Sting
International Caps/Goals : - 62/16

Gadocha would be part of the Polish squad which finished third in the 1974 World Cup. In the tournament, it is alleged that Argentina offered the Poland squad a bonus should they beat Italy in the final group match which would ensure the Argentines progress. Gadocha allegedly pocketed the money meant for the whole side, an allegation he denies.

246. Wlodzmierz Lubanski   Poland (2)

Poland vs USA   4-0   20/03/1973

Clubs : Gornik Zabrze, Lokeren, Valenciennes, Stade Quimperois
International Caps/Goals : - 75/48

Like Gadocha, Lubanski was part of the 1972 Olympic Gold medal winning side, however, he missed the 1974 World Cup. He remains the second highest goalscorer for the Polish national team having been taken over by Robert Lewandowski.

247. Trevor Hockey Wales (15)

Wales vs Poland   2-0   28/03/1973

Clubs : Bradford City, Nottingham Forest, Newcastle United, Birmingham City, Sheffield United, Norwich City, Aston Villa, Athlone Town, San Diego Jaws, Las Vegas Quicksilvers, San Jose Earthquakes, Ashton United

International Caps/ Goals : - 9/1

Hockey is the very definition of a journeyman footballer having represented 12 clubs in an 18 year career. Whilst at Birmingham City, Hockey released a single called 'Happy Cos I'm Blue' and was immensely popular at most of the clubs he represented due to his hard working tough tackling style of play and his beard.

248. George Graham   Scotland (40)

Scotland vs Wales   2-0   12/05/1973

Clubs: Aston Villa, Chelsea, Arsenal, Manchester United, Portsmouth, Crystal Palace, California Surf

International Caps / Goals : - 12/3

Graham was part of the Arsenal side which won a league and cup double in 1971 and also managed them to a cup double in 1992/1993, where dour football and a lack of goals led them to be dubbed 'Boring, Boring Arsenal'. Graham would be banned from management for a period for accepting a payment from agent Rune Hauge of £425,000.[xix]

249. Kenny Dalglish Scotland (41)

Scotland vs Northern Ireland 1-2 16/05/1973

Clubs : Celtic, Liverpool

International Caps/Goals : - 102/30

Dalglish is one of the most trophied players and managers in British football, having one four titles with Celtic as a player, six with Liverpool (and a further two as manager) and a Premier League as manager of Blackburn Rovers. Added to that he would win three European Cups and remains the most capped Scotland player and joint top goalscorer. Liverpool's Anfield has a stand named for Dalglish.

250. Martin Peters England (46)

England vs Scotland 1-0 19/05/1973

See Entry 230

251. Allan Clarke   England (47)

England vs Czechoslovakia   1-1   27/05/1973

Clubs : Walsall, Fulham, Leicester City, Leeds
United, Barnsley
International Caps/Goals : - 19/10

Allan Clarke formed part of the successful Leeds
United team of the sixties and seventies and
acquired the moniker, 'Sniffer' for his ability to sniff
out goalscoring chances. Clarke played in the 1975
European Cup final defeat against Bayern Munich,
where a tackle from Beckenbauer looked to give a
penalty to the English side which was not given.

252. Wlodzmierz Lubanski   Poland (3)

Poland   vs England   2-0   06/06/1973

See Entry 246

1974 – 1988
Big Match Temperament

Lubanski's absence from the Poland squad for three years would ensure that the trophy would not see the 1974 World Cup and the Iron Curtain would allow Eastern European sides a time to gain the title with the trophy passing through many of the nations in the region. The trophy would, however, return to the World Cup in 1978 and 1986, where it would be contested and won in the final by Argentina (with Daniel Bertoni and Jorge Burruchaga the recipients).

Countries

Poland
Hungary
USSR
Greece
Yugoslavia
Spain
Italy
France
Netherlands
Argentina
Brazil
Uruguay
Chile

Peru
East Germany
West Germany
Argentina

Players

253.Stanislaw Terlecki   Poland (4)

Poland vs Cyprus   5-0   31/10/1976

Clubs : - Gwardia Warszawa, Lodzki KS, Golden
Bay Earthquakes, New York Cosmos, Legia
Warsaw, Polonia Warsaw
International Caps / Goals : - 29/7

Terlecki considered that he had been 'retired' from
football in Poland by the government following an
incident at an airport and a meeting with the Pope.
He campaigned against the Communist dictatorship
and this led to emigration to the United States.

254.Tibor Nyilasi   Hungary (11)

Hungary vs Poland 2-1   13/04/1977

Clubs : - Ferencvaros, Austria Vienna
International Caps / Goals : - 70/32

Nyilasi appeared for Hungary at two World Cups and would win two Hungarian titles as a player with Ferencvaros and one as a manager, and also three Austrian Bundesliga titles with Austria Vienna. He would finish as top scorer in the Hungarian and Austrian leagues on one occasion each, being the second top scorer in European football in 1981.

255.Istvan Kovacs   Hungary (12)

Hungary vs Czechoslovakia   2-0   20/04/1977

Clubs : Salgotarjan, Vasas SC, Tatabanya, Eger ES, FC Malley
International Caps / Goals : - 10/1

Kovacs only international goal would be a 'Last Goal Wins' Trophy winner, and he would end his career in Switzerland in 1987.Whilst at Vasas he would win the only title of his career in the 1976 – 77 season.

256.David Kipiani   USSR (1)

USSR vs Hungary   1-2   30/04/1977

USSR's First 'Last Goal Wins' Trophy

Clubs :- Locomotive Tbilisi, Dinamo Tbilisi
International Caps / Goals : - 19/7

Part of the Dinamo Tbilisi side which would win the European Cup Winners Cup in 1981, Kipiani is well regarded in his native Georgia as one of their finest ever players. He would manage Dinamo Tbilisi on four occasions, and also the independent Georgia twice.

257.Dimitrios Papaioanou   Greece (3)

Greece   vs USSR   1-0   10/05/1977

Clubs : Veria, AEK Athens, New York Pancyprian Freedoms

International Caps / Goals : - 61/21

Papaioanou's career would last into his 40s, playing in the United States for the rather grandly named New York Pancyprian Freedoms. His 18 year spell at AEK would see him win five Greek titles and finish as top scorer in the Greek league on two occasions.

258.Lazlo Fazekas Hungary (13)

Hungary vs Greece 3-0   28/05/1977

Clubs : Ujpesti Dozsa, Royal Antwerp, Sint Truidense
International Caps / Goals : - 92/24

Fazekas won Olympic gold for the Hungarian national team in 1968 and would also take part in the 1978 and 1982 World Cup, scoring twice in a 10-1 win over El Salvador. He remains the third most capped player for the Hungarian national team.

259.Dusan Nikolic   Yugoslavia (5)

Yugoslavia vs Hungary   4-3   05/10/1977

Clubs : Red Star Belgrade, Bolton Wanderers, Teteks Tetovo, OFK Beograd
International Caps/Goals : - 4/1

Nikolic had a short international career and would spend two seasons playing in England for Bolton Wanderers where his promise was cut short by injury. His time at Red Star would see him win three Yugoslav titles. Nikolic passed away on the 15th December 2018.

260.Zoran Filipovic   Yugoslavia (6,7)

Yugoslavia vs Romania   6-4   13/11/1977 (held for 2 games)

Clubs : Red Star Belgrade, Club Brugge, Benfica, Boavista
International Caps/ Goals : - 13/2

Filipovic is Red Star's leading goalscorer in European football, and third leading scorer overall and would become the first coach of an independent Montenegro. Whilst with Red Star he would win three Yugoslav First Leagues, and would add to that total with two Primera Liga titles at Benfica.

261.Ruben Andres Cano   Spain (12)

Spain vs Yugoslavia1-0   30/11/1977

Clubs : Atlanta, Elche, Atletico Madrid, Tenerife, Rayo Vallecano
International Caps / Goals : - 12/4

Cano was born in Argentina to Spanish parents and although starting his career in Argentina, he would choose to represent Spain including in the 1978 World Cup. Cano's time at Atletico would see him score a goal nearly every other game with 82 in 168 appearances.

262.Marco Tardelli Italy (10)

Italy vs Spain   1-2   25/01/1978

Clubs : Pisa, Como, Juventus, Internazionale, St Gallen

International Caps/Goals : - 81/6

Tardelli is well known for his celebration following his goal in the 1982 World Cup Final which brought him to tears in an outpouring of emotion. He is one of few players to win all four major European competitions and would also win five league titles with Juventus.

263.Michel Platini   France (9,10)

Francevs Italy   2-2   08/02/1978 (held for 2 games)

Clubs : Nancy, Saint Etienne, Juventus

International Caps/Goals : - France 72/41 Kuwait 1/0

Platini is the top scorer in European Championships with 9 goals, despite having only appeared in France's victorious 1984 participation in the tournament. He would also reach the semi finals of the 1982 and 1986 World Cups. Platini would win the Ballon d'or in three consecutive seasons from 1983 through to 1985. Later becoming a football administrator and head of UEFA, Platini was banned from football administration by the FIFA Ethics committee. Bizarrely, Platini would also gain an international cap for Kuwait towards the end of his playing career.

264.Christian Dalger   France (11)

France vs Tunisia   2-0   19/05/1978

Clubs : Toulon, Monaco

International Caps/Goals : - 6/2

Dalger would be part of the Monaco side which would win Ligue 1 in 1978 and would be involved in football as a manager and a player for nearly fifty years including a spell as manager of the Malian national team. Dalger's goal in this pre-World Cup friendly would have a slight hint of fortune, with an attempted clearance by the Tunisian defender ricocheting over Dalger's arm leaving him free to slot home eight metres from goal.

265.Renato Zaccarelli   Italy (11)
Italy vs France   2-1   02/06/1978

Clubs : Catania, Torino, Novara, Verona
International Caps/Goals : - 25/2

Zaccarelli's winner in the 1978 World Cup fixture against France in the group stages would come from the bench as with his five other appearances in the tournament. The 54th minute goal struck into the bottom corner from inside the box was his last for Italy, his only other coming in a 6-1 victory over Finland in the qualifiers for the tournament.

266.Roberto Bettega   Italy (12,13)

Italy vs Argentina   1-0   10/06/1978 (held for 2 games)

Clubs : Juventus, Varese, Toronto Blizzard
International Caps/Goals : 42/19

A member of the Italy squad in the the 1978 World Cup, where this goal would be scored, he would gain the title in the next match also. Selected in the Italy Euro 1980 squad after being top scorer in Serie A that season, Bettega would miss Italy's triumph in the 1982 World Cup through injury.

267.Paolo Rossi   Italy (14)
Italy vs Austria   1-0   18/06/1978

Clubs : Juventus, Como, Vicenza, Perugia, Milan, Hellas Verona
International Caps/Goals : 48/20

Voted the second best player in the 1978 World Cup, Rossi would be banned from football for his involvement in the 1980 Totonero match fixing scandal, having his three year ban reduced to two on appeal. This would allow him to star in Italy's 1982 World Cup triumph and finish with the Golden Boot in the tournament, subsequently winning the Ballon d'or in the same season. He would secure two Italian titles and a European Cup in his playing career.

268.Arie Haan   Netherlands (8)

Netherlands vs Italy   2-1   21/06/1978

Clubs : Ajax, Anderlecht, Standard Liege, PSV, Seiko
International Caps/Goals : - 35/6

Haan would appear in two World Cup finals for the Netherlands finishing as runner up on both occasions and would also form part of the Ajax side who would win three consecutive European Cups in the seventies. A move to Belgium followed where he would win the European Cup Winners Cup twice with Anderlecht and finish as runner up with Standard. After retirement, Haan has had a nomadic managerial career, taking in the national teams of China, Cameroon and Albania, and also managing clubs in Belgium, Austria, Iran, Germany, Cyprus, Greece and his native Netherlands.

269.Daniel Bertoni   Argentina (15,16)

Argentina vs Netherlands 3-1   25/06/1978
World Cup Final (held for two games)

Clubs : Quilmes, Independiente, Sevilla, Fiorentina,
Napoli, Udinese
International Caps/Goals : - 31/12

Sealing the 1978 World Cup for Argentina and the
'Last Goal Wins' Trophy for himself following a
somewhat fortunate one-two with Mario Kempes,
Bertoni would also claim one Argentine title and
three Copa Libertadores trophies in his career. In
2018, Bertoni was inducted into the Fiorentina Hall
of Fame. Following the World Cup victory, he
would retain the title in a rematch of the World Cup
final in 1979 before facing a two year absence from
the national side.

270.Roberto Diaz   Argentina (17)

Argentina vs West Germany   2-1   01/01/1981

Clubs : Chacanta Juniors, Estudiantes, Racing Club,
Tampico Madero, Tigres, UANL, America, Leon
International Caps/Goals : 6/1

Diaz would form part of the 1979 Argentina squad for the Copa America which would see the World Champions finish bottom of a group including Brazil and Bolivia. He would end his career in Mexico and remains one of Racing Clubs top scorers of the last forty years.

271. De Freitas Edevaldo   Brazil (19)

Brazil vs Argentina 1-1   04/01/1981

Clubs : Fluminense, Internacional, Vasco Da Gama, Porto, Botafogo, Nautico, Bangu, Vila Nova, America, Castelo, Izabelense, Portuguesa da Ilha, Mesquita
International Caps/Goals : 18/1

This goal would come in the 1980/81 Mundalito tournament to commemorate 50 years since the first World Cup in Uruguay, Edevaldo would represent his country the following year in the World Cup in Spain. His only period outside of South America would see him win the Portuguese title with Porto.

272. Ze Sergio   Brazil (20)

Brazil vs West Germany   4-1   07/01/1981

Clubs : Sao Paulo, Santos, Vasco Da Gama, Kashiwa Reysol
International Caps/Goals : 25/5

A member of the Brazil 1978 World Cup squad but injured for the 1982 edition, Ze Sergio would go on to play and manage in Japan. His daughter, Thaissa Presti won the bronze medal in the 4x100m relay in the Beijing Olympics in 2008.

273.Waldemar Victorino   Uruguay (8)

Uruguay vs Brazil   2-1   10/01/1981

Clubs : Cerro, Progreso, River Plate (Uruguay), Nacional, Deportivo Cali, Cagliari, Newell's Old Boys, Colon de Santa Fe, LDU Portoviejo, Sport Boys

International Caps/Goals : - 33/15

Victorino's career would take him to six different countries and also see him win the Mundialito and be top scorer in the tournament to commemorate the 50th Anniversary of the World Cup, which this game formed part of. This goal a stooping header from within the six yard box, would secure the tournament for Uruguay.

274.Nelson Agresta   Uruguay (9,10,11)

Uruguay vs Chile   2-1   29/04/1981 (held for 3 games)

Clubs : Liverpool (Uruguay), Estudiantes, Defensor Sporting, Argentinos Juniors, Nacional, River Plate (Uruguay) Sud America, San Luis de Quillota, LDU Portoviejo

International Caps/Goals : - 34/1

Subsequent goalless draws against Peru and Paraguay ensure that Agresta held the title more times than he has scored international goals. He formed part of the 1983 Copa America winning side after also appearing in the 1979 edition.

275.Fernando Morena   Uruguay (12)

Uruguay vs Paraguay   3-0   09/06/1983

Clubs : Racing Montevideo, River Plate (Uruguay), Penarol, Rayo Vallecano, Valencia, Flamengo, Boca Juniors

International Caps/Goals : - 53/22

Morena remains the top scorer in Uruguayan league football having scored 203 goals in 196 games for Penarol, winning six league titles in the process and being the top scorer in the Uruguayan league for six consecutive seasons. In 1978, he scored seven goals in one game for Penarol, even missing a penalty in the last minute.

276. Arsenio Luzardo   Uruguay (13)

Uruguay vs Peru   1-1   18/07/1983

Clubs : Nacional, Recreativo de Huelva, LG
Cheetahs, US Biskra
International Caps/Goals : 11/2

Luzardo would, like Morena, be part of the the 1983
Copa America winning side for Uruguay. He would
also win two Uruguayan league titles and a Copa
Libertadores title in the 1980s before moving to
South Korea.

277. Juan Carlos Orellana   Chile (12)

Chile vs Uruguay   1-2   01/09/1983

Clubs : Green Cross Temuco, Colo Colo, O'Higgins,
Union Espanola, Deportes Antofagasta
International Caps/Goals : - 17/7

Orellana would score the first goal for Colo Colo in
their new stadium in 1975, the Estadio Monumental.
He would win the Chilean title and Cup during his
spell with Colo Colo and represent the national side
in the 1983 Copa America.

278. Jorge Aravena   Chile (13)

Chile vs Venezuela   5-0   08/09/1983

Clubs : Universidad Catolica, Santiago Morning, Naval, Real Valladolid, Deportivo Cali, Puebla, Portuguesa, Union Espanola, Audax Italiano.
International Caps/Goals : - 36/22

A goal scoring midfielder, Aravena would win the Mexican Primera Division with Puebla and finish top scorer in the Colombian Primera Division in 1987 and in the qualifiers for the 1986 World Cup. Following a 1-0 win against Mexico in 1984, he would hold the 'Last Goal Wins' Trophy for a further two games, against Paraguay and Finland.

279.Juan Carlos Letelier   Chile (14,15)

Chile vs Uruguay   2-0   11/09/1983 (held for two games)

Clubs : Santiago Wanderers, Audax Italiano, Cobreloa, Independiente Medellin, Deportes La Serena, Internacional, Cruz Azul, Deportes Antofagasta, Universitario, Caracas, Sporting Cristal

International Caps/Goals : - 57/18

Letelier and Aravena share the title between themselves for 18 months from 1983-1985. Letelier was something of a nomad throughout his career, playing in Chile, Colombia, Brazil, Mexico, Peru and Venezuela, picking up titles in Peru and Chile. He would represent Chile in the 1982 Spanish World Cup.

280.Jorge Aravena   Chile (16,17,18)

Chile vs Mexico   1-0   28/10/1984 (held for 3 games)

See Entry 278

281.Juan Carlos Letelier   Chile (19)

Chile vs Colombia   1-1   21/02/1985

See Entry 279

282. Franco Navarro   Peru (8)
Peru vs Chile 2-1   24/02/1985

Clubs : Municipal, Sporting Cristal, Deportivo Cali, Independiente, Tecos UAG, Wettingen, Union Santa Fe, Carlos A Manucci, Alianza Lima
International Caps/Goals : - 56/16

Navarro would represent Peru at the 1982 World Cup and later coach the national side in 2006. His career was nearly ended by a broken leg in a key World Cup qualifier against Argentina in the June of 1985.

283.Wilmer Cabrera Uruguay
(14)

Uruguay vs Peru   2-2   27/02/1985

Clubs : Nacional, Milonarios, Valencia, Nice, Sporting de Gijon, Necaxa, Nacional, Huracan Buceo, Rampla Juniors, River Plate Montevideo

International Caps/Goals : - 26/6

Not to be confused with the Colombian footballer of the same name, Cabrera would form part of the 1983 Copa America winning side for Uruguay and the 1986 World Cup squad.

284.Venancio Ramos Uruguay
(15)

Uruguay vs Ecuador   2-1   10/03/1985

Clubs : Penarol, Lens, Independiente, Racing Montevideo, Nacional, Defensor Sporting, El Tanque Sisley

International Caps/Goals : - 41/5

Another who would be part of both the 1983 Copa America winning side and 1986 World Cup Squad, Ramos would also win four Uruguayan titles and a Copa Libertadores whilst at Penarol. Since retirement he has been heavily involved in beach football, where he has coached the Uruguayan side to the World Cup.

285.Enzo Francescoli   Uruguay (16)

Uruguay vs Ecuador   2-0   31/03/1985

Clubs : Wanderers, River Plate, RC Paris, Marseille, Cagliari, Torino
International Caps/Goals : - 73/17

Francescoli would win the Copa America three times with Uruguay in 1983,1987 and 1995 and also win five titles with River Plate and the Copa Libertadores. His short time with Marseille included a French title and a run to the semi finals of the European Cup, it also inspired Zinedine Zidane, who has named one of his sons for Francescoli.

286.Venancio Ramos   Uruguay (17)

Uruguay vs Chile   2-1   07/04/1985

See Entry 284

287.Jose Toure   France (12)

France vs Uruguay 2-0   21/08/1985

Clubs : Nantes, Bordeaux, Monaco
International Caps/Goals : 16/4

Toure would win three French titles throughout his career with Nantes and Bordeaux, but his career would end before the age of thirty due to personal issues involving alcohol and drugs, culminating in his arrest and imprisonment for four months.

288.Ronald Kreer   East Germany (1)

East Germany vs France   2-0   11/09/1985

East Germany's First 'Last Goal Wins' Trophy

Clubs : Lokomotive Leipzig, VfB Leipzig
International Caps/Goals : - 65/2

Although the tenth most capped East German player of all time, Kreer's international career would end with the fall of the Berlin Wall. This low strike which squirmed underneath the French keeper, would secure victory for East Germany.

289.Haris Skoro   Yugoslavia (8)

Yugoslavia vs East Germany   1-2   28/09/1985

Clubs : Zeljeznicar Sarajevo, Dinamo Zagreb,
Torino, Zurich, Baden
International Caps/Goals : - 15/4

Born in Sarajevo, Bosnia, Skoro would form part of
the Zeljeznicar team to reach the Semi Finals of the
1984-85 Uefa Cup. A consolation goal for
Yugoslavia, Skoro would perform an acrobatic
volley in the six yard area for this goal.

290.Zlatko Vujovic   Yugoslavia (9)
Yugoslavia vs Austria   3-0   16/10/1985

Clubs : Hajduk Split, Bordeaux, Cannes, Paris Saint
Germain, Sochaux, Nice
Interational Caps/Goals : - 70/27

Vujovic would spend most of his career in France
where he would play at Bordeaux with his identical
twin brother Zoran. In the 1987 semifinals of the
Uefa Cup Winners Cup, Zlatko deemed himself to
nervous to take a spot kick in the shoot out and sent
his brother to take it in his place. He missed.[xx]

291.Michel Platini   France (13,14)
France vs Yugoslavia   2-0   16/11/1985 (held
for 2 games)

See Entry 263

292.Jean-Pierre Papin   France (15)
France vs Canada   1-0   01/06/1986

Clubs : Valenciennes, Club Brugge, Marseille, Milan, Bayern Munich, Bordeaux, Guingamp, Saint Pierre (Reunion)
International Caps/Goals : - 54/30

Papin is often overlooked where the discussion of great French players is concerned, the large part of his career coming between the end of Platini's French side and the World Cup winning side of 1998. A key part of the Marseille side at the turn of the eighties and nineties, he would win six consecutive titles, four with Marseille and two with AC Milan where he also won a European Cup. A Uefa Cup win with Bayern Munich also followed, however, his time there was interrupted by injury.

293.Luis Fernandez France (16)
Francevs USSR   1-1   05/06/1986

Clubs : Paris Saint Germain, RC Paris, Cannes
International Caps/Goals : - 60/6

Born in Spain, Fernandez moved to France as a young child and chose to represent the French national team. Fernandez formed part of the French midfield which won Euro 84 and reached the semifinals of the 1986 World Cup. As a manager, he took charge of PSG on two occasions, winning the European Cup Winners Cup in 1996.

294.Dominique Rocheteau   France (17)
Francevs Hungary   3-0   09/06/1986

Clubs: Saint Etienne, Paris Saint Germain, Toulouse.
International Caps/Goals : - 49/15

Rocheteau would also be part of the Euro 84 winning squad for France and would score in three World Cups for his country. Following retirement he has starred in films, commercials and moved into football administration for Saint Etienne and the French Football Federation.

295.Yannick Stopyra   France (18)

Francevs Italy   2-0   17/06/1986

Clubs: Sochaux, Rennes, Toulouse, Bordeaux, Cannes, Metz, Mulhouse
International Caps/Goals : - 33/11

Stopyra's strike in the 56th minute ended Italy's hopes of defending their World Cup in the second round, France would continue on to a third place finish. Stopyra's domestic career would see him remain in France with his most successful period coming at Sochaux leading them to second place in 1979/80.

296.Michel Platini France (19)

Francevs Brazil   1-1   21/06/1986

See Entry 263

297.Rudi Voller West Germany (11)

West Germany vs France   2-0   25/06/1986

Clubs : Kickers Offenbach, 1860 Munich, Werder Bremen, Roma, Marseille, Bayer Leverkusen. International Caps/Goals : - 90/47

Voller is one of four people to reach the final of the World Cup as a player and a manager, securing runners up spots in 1986 and 2002, and being part of the victorious West German side of 1990. It was in 1990 that he would find his hair full of Frank Rijkaard's spit following an altercation between the two, resulting in the sending off of both players. A prolific goalscorer, Voller would win the newly styled Champions League with Marseille in 1993.

298.Jorge Burruchaga   Argentina (18,19)

Argentina vs West Germany   3-2   29/06/1986
World Cup Final (held for two games)

Clubs : Arsenal di Sarandi, Independiente, Nantes,
Valenciennes

International Caps/Goals : - 57/13

Burruchaga's winner in the 1986 World Cup Final, a
breakaway in the 84th minute would secure
Argentina's second world title and the 'Last Goal
Wins' Trophy for Burruchaga. Burruchaga would
also finish as runner up in the 1990 World Cup. His
later career would see him take part in the
controversial 1993 fixture between Marseille and
Valenciennes, where Valenciennes would suffer a 1-
0 defeat to ease Marseilles chances in the
Champions League final.

1988 – 2002
Uni Arge's Barmy Army

European sides would again hold onto the 'Last Goal Wins' Trophy for much of the period at the end of the century, with the tiny Faroe Islands standing in contrast to massive Russia and Brazil in winning the title. Pablo Bengoechea would hold the title for a period of four years following Uruguay's exit from the 1990 World Cup, failing to make an appearance for the Uruguayan national side in four years. The era would end in South America as it started with the trophy going to the eventual World Cup winners Brazil, and their famous strike force of Ronaldo, Rivaldo and Ronaldinho,

Countries

Argentina
Brazil
England
Uruguay
Spain
Belgium
Denmark
Germany
France
Faroe Islands
Yugoslavia
Russia

Poland
Scotland
Netherlands
Slovenia
Chile
Venezuela

Players

299.Claudio Caniggia   Argentina
(20,21,22,23)

Argentina vs Chile 1-0   02/07/1989 (held for 4 games)

Clubs : - River Plate, Hellas Verona, Atalanta, Roma, Benfica, Boca Juniors, Dundee, Rangers, Qatar
International Caps/Goals : - 50/16

Caniggia was banned for cocaine use in 1993, like his compatriot, Diego Maradona, a year earlier. In the 2002 World Cup, he was sent off whilst still on the bench in the game against Sweden and he would return to football in 2012 to play for Wembley FC. He would win one Argentinian title, a Copa Libertadores and one Scottish Premiership during his career.

300.Romario   Brazil (20,21,22)

Brazil vs Argentina 2-0   12/07/1989 (held for 3 games)

Clubs : Vasco Da Gama, PSV, Barcelona, Flamengo, Valencia, Fluminense, Al Sadd, Miami, Adelaide United, America RJ
Internation Caps/Goals : - 70/55

Romario is currently a politician in his native Brazil but had an incredibly successful 24 year career in football. He was named player of the tournament in Brazil's world cup triumph of 1994 and Fifa World Player of the Year in the same year. Despite a rocky personal relationship with strike partner, Bebeto in the 1994 tournament, Romario would form part of the rocking baby celebration. A fantastic career full of team honours and individual records, including three consecutive league titles at PSV, the World Cup in 1994 and two editions of the Copa America.

301.Bismarck   Brazil (23,24)

Brazil vs Japan   1-0   23/07/1989 (held for 2 games)

Clubs : Vasco da Gama, Verdy Kawasaki, Kashima Antlers, Fluminense, Goias, Vissel Kobe
International Caps/Goals : - 13/1

Bismarck (named after the German Chancellor Otto von Bismarck) would score his only international goal against Japan, where he would later spend the majority of his football career. Also like Romario, he would be part of 1989 Copa America winning side. A subsequent 0-0 draw with Yugoslavia in his next appearance would see Bismarck hold the 'Last Goal Wins' Trophy for a further game.

302. Gary Lineker   England (48)
England vs Brazil   1-0   28/03/1990

Clubs : Leicester City, Everton, Barcelona, Tottenham Hotspur, Nagoya Grampus Eight
International Caps/Goals : - 80/48

Lineker famously never received a booking in his footballing career and is now a television presenter in the UK. He also sells crisps and has a legion of twitter followers who say Gary Lineker 'shat on the pitch' following an incident in the 1990 World Cup against Ireland where he did just that. Despite his prolific goalscoring record, domestic titles were few for Lineker, limited to a Second Division title with Leicester, a Spanish and English Cup and also the European Cup Winners Cup with Barcelona in 1989. He received the Golden Boot in the 1986 World Cup with six goals and remains England's record goalscorer at World Cup tournaments.

303.Paul Gascoigne England (49)
England vs Czechoslovakia   4-2   25/04/1990

Clubs : Newcastle United, Tottenham Hotspur,
Lazio, Rangers, Middlesbrough, Everton, Burnley,
Gansu Tianma, Boston United
International Caps/Goals :- 57/10

Still widely loved in England, Gascoigne is regarded
as 'the most naturally gifted English Midfielder of
his generation'[xxi] Gascoigne is also widely known
for his bizarre antics, including hiding fish in
teammates cars, turning up to armed sieges with
fishing rods and fried chicken and playing tennis
prior to a World Cup semi final with American
tourists. Much like Lineker, his ability did not
translate into domestic trophy success, with two
titles in Scotland to add to an English and Scottish
Cup.

304.Gary Lineker   England (50)
England vs Denmark   1-0   15/05/1990

See entry 303.

305.Jose Perdomo   Uruguay (18,19)

Uruguay vs England   2-1   22/05/1990 (held
for 2 games)

Clubs : Penarol, Genoa, Coventry City, Real Betis, Gimnasia y Esgrima La Plata

International Caps / Goals : - 27/2

Perdomo was largely unsuccessful in his time in Italy, with the manager of rival team, Sampdoria, stating "Se io sciolgo il mio cane, lui gioca meglio di Perdomo" (if I release my dog, he plays better than Perdomo).[xxii] A year later, Perdomo had returned to South America after short spells with Coventry and Betis.

308.Pablo Bengoechea   Uruguay (20)

Uruguay vs Belgium   1-3   17/06/1990

Clubs : Montevideo Wanderers, Sevilla, Gimnasia La Plata, Penarol

International Caps/ Goals : - 43/6

A late side footed volley from the penalty spot would only be a consolation for Uruguay in this World Cup fixture with Belgium. Bengoechea wouldn't play for the national side for four years until after the next world cup. Bengoechea would score in the finals of two of Uruguay's Copa America triumphs, in 1987 and 1995.

309.Dario Silva   Uruguay (21)

Uruguay vs Peru   1-0   19/10/1994

Clubs : Defensor, Penarol, Cagliari, Espanyol, Malaga, Sevilla, Portsmouth
International Caps / Goals : - 49/14

Silva's career would be ended by a serious car accident which would require a leg amputation following his time at Portsmouth, where he also fractured a skull in the accident. He would play in Uruguay's unsuccessful 2002 World Cup campaign, which would see them eliminated along with France in the group stages.

310. Donato   Spain (12,13)

Spain vs Uruguay   2-2   18/01/1995 (held for two games)

Clubs : America, Vasco Da Gama, Atletico Madrid, Deportivo La Coruna
International Caps/Goals : - 12/3

Born in Brazil, Donato represented his adopted home country in Spain, where he represented two sides including Deportivo where he won La Liga in 2000 at the age of 38. He would become part of the Euro 96 squad for Spain, appearing in one match.

311. Marc Degryse Belgium (12)
Belgium vs Spain   1-1   29/03/1995

Clubs: Club Brugge, Anderlecht, Sheffield
Wednesday, PSV, Gent, Germinal Beerschot
International Caps/Goals : - 63/23

Degryse would appear in both the 1990 and 1994
World Cups for Belgium, scoring twice in the
process. He would win five Belgian titles in his
career and an Eredivisie at PSV. Whilst at Sheffield
Wednesday, Degryse had a cameo appearance in
the Sheffield based film 'The Full Monty', but it
didn't make it to the final cut.

312. Gunther Schepens Belgium (13)
Belgium vs USA   2-0   22/04/1995

Clubs : Gent, Standard Liege, Karlsruher SC, Gent,
SC Bregenz

International Caps/Goals : - 13/3

During his career, Schepens principle achievement
was finishing as runner up in the Belgian top
division with Standard. Following his retirement,
Schepens has worked as a pundit on Belgian TV,
notably during the 2010 World Cup, and further
moved into coaching and scouting with his
hometown club of Gent.

313. Enzo Scifo Belgium (14)

Belgium vs FYR Macedonia   5-0   07/06/1995

Clubs : Anderlecht, Internazionale, Bordeaux, Auxerre, Torino, AS Monaco, Charleroi

International Caps/Goals : - 84/18

Scifo would be one of Belgium's finest midfielders, appearing in four World Cups and winning four Belgian titles and one French Title. In 1986, with Belgium's fourth place finish in the World Cup he was noted as the Best Young Player. Scifo retired due to injury at the age of 36.

314. Kim Vilfort   Denmark (1)

Denmark vs Belgium   3-1   06/09/1995
(held for two games)

Denmark's First 'Last Goal Wins' Trophy

Clubs : Skovlunde IF, BK Frem, Lille, Brondby

International Caps/Goals : - 77/14

Vilfort would represent Denmark in three European Championships being part of the victorious 1992 side in Sweden. Sadly, his daughter would be seriously ill with leukemia at the time of the tournament, passing away shortly after. His time at Brondby would see him win seven Danish titles.

315. Michael Laudrup   Denmark (2)
Denmark vs Armenia   3-1   15/11/1995

Clubs : KB, Brondby, Lazio, Juventus, Barcelona, Real Madrid, Vissel Kobe, Ajax.
International Caps/Goals : - 104/37

One of the finest Danish footballers in history, Laudrup would not form part of the Euro 92 championship winning side having withdrawn from international selection in 1990. He would appear in the 1984, 1988 and 1996 editions of the tournament, along with the 1986 and 1998 World Cups. Domestically, Laudrup would win five La Liga titles (four with Barcelona, one with Real Madrid), one Serie A, one European Cup and one Eredivisie title.

316. Oliver Bierhoff   Germany (4)

Germany vs Denmark   2-0   27/03/1996

Clubs : Bayer Uerdingen, Hamburg, Borussia Monchengladback, Austria Salzburg, Ascoli, Udinese, Milan, Monaco, Chievo

International Caps/Goals: - 70/37

Scorer of the first Golden goal, i.e a goal scored in sudden death extra time, in international football against Czech Republic in the final of Euro 96, Bierhoff would also come on as a substitute in Germany's 2002 World Cup final defeat. His only domestic triumph came for AC Milan, winning Serie A in 1998-99.

317. Jurgen Klinsmann   Germany (5)

Germany vs Netherlands   1-0   24/04/1996

Clubs : Stuttgart Kickers, Vfb Stuttgat, Internazionale, AS Monaco, Tottenham Hotspur, Bayern Munich, Sampdoria. Orange County Blue Star

International Caps/Goals : - West Germany 26/7 Germany 82/40

Fondly remembered in English football for his time at Tottenham Hotspur where he would celebrate goals with a dive (in criticism of those who suggested he went down too easily), Klinnsmann would later go on to manage the German and United States national sides. Internationally, he would represent Germany (and previously West Germany) at six major tournaments, scoring in each and is the sixth highest World Cup goalscorer. His son has been capped by the United States at youth level.

318. Mehmet Scholl   Germany (6)

Germany vs Northern Ireland   1-1
       29/05/1996

Clubs : Karlsruhe, Bayern Munich

International Caps/Goals : - 36/8

Scholl was a mainstay of the Bayern Munich side throughout the 1990s and into the 2000s. As a result, he won eight Bundesliga titles, five German cups, one Champions League and one Uefa Cup. He occasionally presents a radio show playing his favourite rock and indie tracks.

319. Laurent Blanc   France (20)

France vs Germany   1-0   01/06/1996

Clubs : Montpellier, Napoli, Nimes, Saint Etienne, Auxerre, Barcelona, Marseille, Internazionale, Manchester United

International Caps/Goals : - 97/16

Blanc would win both the 1998 World Cup and Euro 2000 with France and regularly planted a kiss on keeper, Fabian Barthez's bald head. He would score the first Golden Goal in a World Cup (sudden death extra time, a true manner of 'last goal wins') against Paraguay in 1998. Although representing many of Europe's top clubs, he would only win two league titles in his career, at Auxerre in 1996 and Manchester United in 2003.

320. Mickael Madar France (21)
France vs Armenia 2-0   05/06/1996 (no further international appearances)

Clubs : Sochaux, Laval, Cannes, Monaco, Deportivo, Everton, Paris Saint Germain, Creteil
International Caps/Goals : - 3/1

Madar formed part of the French squad for Euro 96 but would not make an appearance in the tournament. Madar broke a leg whilst at Deportivo which disrupted his career, signing for Everton shortly after.

321. Christophe Dugarry France (22)
France vs Romania   1-0   10/06/1996

Clubs: Bordeaux, Milan, Barcelona, Marseille, Birmingham City, Qatar SC
International Caps/Goals : - 55/8

Dugarry is another player who would be a member of both the 1998 World Cup and Euro 2000 winning sides for France. Following his retirement in 2005, he would be a tv pundit for Canal + for over ten years.

322. Jose Luis Caminero   Spain (14,15)

Spain vs France   1-1   15/06/1996 (held for two games, no further appearances for Spain)

Clubs: Real Madrid, Valladolid, Atletico Madrid
International Caps/Goals : - 21/8

Caminero's equaliser against France in the Euro 96 group stages would secure their passageway to the quarter finals, where a nil-nil draw against England and subsequent penalty defeat would ensure that he kept the 'Last Goal Wins' Trophy. Caminero would not make an appearance for Real Madrid's senior team, but would win the double with cross city rivals Atletico in 1996.

323. Uni Arge

Faroe Islands vs Spain   2-6   04/09/1996

Faroe Islands First 'Last Goal Wins' Trophy

Clubs : HB Torshavn, Leiftur, FC Aarhus, IA
Akranes
International Caps/Goals : 37/8

Arge has had a more productive retirement than
football career, releasing several books on Faroese
culture and politics, releasing three albums and
starring in several films. Arge scored the first ever
competitive goal for the Faroe Islands in 1993
against Cyprus.

324. Dragan Stojkovic   Yugoslavia (10)
Yugoslavia vs Faroe Islands   8-1   06/10/1996

Clubs : Radnicki Nis, Red Star Belgrade, Marseille,
Hellas Verona, Nagoya Grampus Eight
International Caps/Goals : - 84/15

Stojkovic would leave Red Star prior to their
European Cup victory against Marseille, appearing
for the French side in the final against them. It is
said that Stojkovic would not take a penalty in the
shootout against his former club. Stojkovic wouldn't
have to wait long for a European Cup, winning with
Marseille two years later.

325. Predrag Mijatovic   Yugoslavia (11)

Yugoslavia vs Czech Republic 1-0 10/11/1996

Clubs : Buducnost, Partizan, Valencia, Real Madrid,
Fiorentina, Levante
International Caps/Goals : - 73/27

Mijatovic would score the winning goal in the 1998
Champions League final, securing victory for Real
Madrid for the first time in 32 years. He appeared
for Yugoslavia in both the 1998 World Cup and at
Euro 2000. This goal assisted Yugoslavia in reaching
the 1998 World Cup finals, Mijatovic finishing with
a lofted ball over the keeper following a one-two
with Vladimir Jugovic.

326. Raul   Spain (16)

Spain vs Yugoslavia 2-0   14/12/1996

Clubs : Real Madrid, Schalke 04, Al Sadd, New York
Cosmos
International Caps/Goals : - 102/44

An illustrious domestic career marked by six La
Liga titles and three Champions Leagues with Real
Madrid, culminating in being runner up in the
Ballon d'or in 2001. Raul's career was unfortunately
coming to a close when his national side, Spain,
began to dominate world football, he was top scorer
for the national side until 2010, and top scorer in
Champions League history until overtaken

by both Cristiano Ronaldo and Lionel Messi.

327. Julen Guerrero   Spain (17)

Spain vs Malta   3-0   18/12/1996

Clubs : Athletic Bilbao
International Caps/Goals : - 41/13

Born in the Basque Country, Guerrero would only represent Athletic Bilbao in his career, and would also appear for the Basque 'national team' eleven times. This goal would be the final of a hat trick against European minnows, Malta

328. Juan Antonio Pizzi   Spain (18)

Spain vs Malta   4-0   12/02/1997

Clubs : Rosario Central, Toluca, Tenerife, Valencia, Barcelona, River Plate, Porto
International Caps/Goals : 22/8

Originally from Argentina, Pizzi spent much of his career in Spain, choosing to represent the national team. Whilst at Barcelona, he would win La Liga and the Cup Winners Cup before entering management, where he would manage Chile to the 2016 Copa America Centenario. He resigned from his role as Saudi Arabia manager in January 2019.

329. Luis Enrique   Spain (19)

Spain vs Faroe Islands   3-1   11/10/1997

Clubs: Sporting Gijon, Real Madrid, Barcelona
International Caps/Goals : 62/12

A winner of La Liga with both Real and Barcelona,
Enrique's international career is principally
remembered for being elbowed by Mauro Tassotti
in the quarter final meeting between the two sides,
losing a pint of blood as a result. As a manager,
Enrique would coach Barcelona to two La Liga titles
and a Champions League.

330. Zinedine Zidane France (23)
France vs Spain   1-0   28/01/1998

Clubs: Cannes, Bordeaux, Juventus, Real Madrid
International Caps/Goals : - 108/31

One of the greatest ever football players, Zidane would win the World Cup and European Championships with France, two titles with Juventus and a title and European Cup with Real Madrid. He would win the Ballon d'or in 1998 and be voted Fifa World Player of the year three times and also be the most expensive footballer following his transfer to Real Madrid from Juventus. Equally, as a manager he has been successful, winning the Champions League three times with Madrid. He could have signed for Blackburn in 1995, but it is reported that the owner of Blackburn responded to Kenny Dalglish (the manager at the time) *'Why do you want to sign Zidane when we have Tim Sherwood?'*. His playing career ended in the 2006 World Cup final where he was sent off for headbutting Marco Materazzi.

331. Marcel Desailly France (24)
France vs Norway   3-3   25/02/1998

Clubs : Nantes, Marseille, Milan, Chelsea, Al Gharafa, Qatar SC
International Caps/Goals : - 116/3

Another member of the World Cup and Euro winning French sides, Desailly was originally born in Ghana and moved to France at the age of 4. A Champions League winner with both Milan and Marseille, he continues to work in the country of his birth for charitable causes.

332. Sergei Yuran   Russia (1)

Russia vs France   1-0   25/03/1998

Russia's First 'Last Goal Wins' Trophy

Clubs : Zorya Voroshilovograd, Dynamo Kyiv,
Benfica, Porto, Spartak Moscow, Millwall, Fortuna
Dusseldorf, Bochum, Sturm Graz

International Caps/Goals : - USSR 12/2 CIS 3/0
Russia 25/5

Having represented the USSR and the
Commonwealth of Independent States, Yuran
would choose to represent Russia over his native
Ukraine. Bizarrely signing for Millwall midseason
in 1996, despite his Spartak side advancing through
the group stages of the Champions League, Yuran
would announce at the press conference with fellow
signing Vasili Kulkov that *'Obviously, we have played
for some of the biggest teams in Europe, but this is the
pinnacle of our careers'.* [xxiii]

333. Vladimir Beschastnykh   Russia (2)

Russia vs Turkey   1-0   22/04/1998

Clubs : Zvezda Moscow, Spartak Moscow, Werder Breman, Racing Santander, Fenerbahce, Kuban, Dinamo Moscow, Oryol, Khimki, Volga Tver, Astana

International Caps/Goals : - 71/26

Beschastnykh would form part of the Russia squads at the 1994 and 2002 World Cups remaining the top scoring Russian national player (excluding goals for the Soviet Union) until 2014 when overtaken by Alexander Kerzhakov.

334. Tomasz Hajto   Poland (5)
Poland vs Russia   3-1   27/05/1998

Clubs : Hutnik Krakow, Gornik Zabrze, MSV Duisburg, Schalke 04, FC Nurnberg, Southampton, Derby, LKS Lodz,
International Caps/Goals : - 62/6

Hajto would have two contracts terminated in England for not meeting standards at both Southampton and Derby. Hajto's post football career would see him escape jail for the manslaughter of an elderly woman who died in a car accident involving the footballer.[xxiv]

335. Rafal Siadaczka   Poland (6)

Poland vs Israel   2-0   18/08/1998

Clubs : Legia Warsaw, Defend Radom, Radomiak Radom, Petrochemia Plock, Widzew Lodz, Austria Vienna, Mazowsze Grojec
International Caps/Goals : - 17/2

Siadaczka would win Polish titles with both Legia Warsaw and Widzew Lodz. He would quit international football due to ongoing problems with diabetes. Both of his international goals for Poland would be 'Last Goal Wins' trophy winning goals.

336. Tomasz Iwan   Poland (7)

Poland vs Bulgaria   3-0   06/09/1998

Clubs : Olimpia Poznan, LKS Lodz, Warta Poznan, Roda JC, Feyenoord, PSV, Trabzonspor, RBC Roosendaal, Admira Wacker, Austria Vienna, Lech Poznan
International Caps/Goals : - 40/4

Iwan would spend much of his career in Netherlands, winning two titles with PSV in 2000 and 2001. This goal in Euro 2000 qualifying saw Iwan run through on the left hand side of the box and dink the ball over the on rushing goalkeeper.

337. Miroslaw Trzeciak   Poland (8)

Poland vs Luxembourg   3-0   10/10/1998

Clubs : Lech Poznan, Young Boys, Maccabi Tel Aviv, LKS Lodz, Osasuna, Poli Ejido

International Caps/Goals : - 22/8

Trzeciak would win three titles at Lech Poznan in the early nineties, which would earn him a move to Switzerland with Young Boys. Returning to Poland with LKS Lodz, he would again earn a move abroad following a title victory, heading to Osasuna in La Liga, where he would later coach their youth team.

338. Rafal Siadczka　　　Poland (9)

Poland vs Malta　　1-0　　03/02/1999

See Entry 335

339. Jonatan Johansson　　　Finland (2)

Finland vs Poland　　1-1　　10/02/1999

Clubs : Pargas IF, TPS, FC Flora, Rangers, Charlton, Norwic City, Malmo, Hibernian, St Johnstone

International Caps/Goals : - 106/22

Johansson would spend much of his career in the British Isles, including six seasons at Charlton in the Premier League. His wife would take part in Celebrity Masterchef in 2018, already a television presenter for 'A Place in the Sun' on the British television station, Channel 4. In 2018, Johansson was appointed manager of Greenock Morton in Scotland.

340. Oliver Neuville   Germany (7)

Germany vs Finland   2-0   31/03/1999

Clubs : Servette, Tenerife, Hansa Rostock, Bayer Leverkusen, Borussia Monchengladbach, Arminia Bielefeld.

International Caps/Goals : - 69/10

Neuville would represent the country of his father, being born in Switzerland himself, in the 2002 and 2006 editions of the World Cup and also in Euro 2008. The majority of his career was spent with Borussia Monchengladbach and Bayer Leverkusen, where he would finish runners up in the Champions League.

341. Don Hutchison   Scotland (42)
Scotland v Germany   1-0   28/04/1999

Clubs : Hartlepool United, Liverpool, West Ham
United, Sheffield United, Everton, Sunderland,
Millwall, Coventry City, Luton
International Caps / Goals : - 26/6

Hutchison was eligible for Scotland through his
father despite being born in England and spending
the entirety of his career in the country. Hutchison
would leave Liverpool following an incident in
Ayia Napa involving flashing his nether regions
behind a Budweiser label.[xxv] Arguably, 1996 was a
very different era.

342. Billy Dodds Scotland (43)
Scotland vs Bosnia   2-1   04/09/1999 (held for
two games)

Clubs : Chelsea, Partick Thistle, Dundee, St
Johnstone, Aberdeen, Dundee United, Rangers
International Caps/Goals : - 26/7

Dodds' twenty yard strike to win the match in
Bosnia would eventually contributed to setting up a
play off for Euro 2000 against the 'Auld Enemy'
England. His career would see two Scottish Cup
victories (one with Dundee, another with Rangers)
and a Scottish title with Rangers.

343. Colin Cameron Scotland (44)

Scotland vs Lithuania   3-0   09/10/1999

Clubs : Raith Rovers, Sligo Rovers, Hearts, Wolverhampton Wanderers, Millwall, Coventry City, Milton Keynes Dons, Dundee, Arbroath, Cowdenbeath, Berwick Rangers
International Caps/Goals : - 28/2

One of Cameron's key football moment came in winning the Scottish League Cup with Raith Rovers, a side in the second tier of Scottish football. He would win the third tier of Scottish football as player manager of Cowdenbeath towards the end of his career.

344 Thierry Henry France (25)
France vs Scotland 2-0   29/03/2000

Clubs : Monaco, Juventus, Arsenal, Barcelona, New York Red Bulls
International Caps/Goals : - 123/51

Originally starting out as a pacey winger, Henry would be turned into a goalscoring striker whilst at Arsenal, where he remains their top goal scorer. A winner of five league titles in his career, a Champions League and also the 1998 World Cup and Euro 2000 internationally, Henry would also win the golden boot for the top scorer on two occasions. His slogan 'va-va voom' from a series of adverts for Renault has entered the Oxford English Dictionary. On signing for New York Red Bulls, Henry professed a great knowledge and understanding of the clubs' history, having been founded all the way back in 1994.

345. David Trezeguet France (25,26)
France v Slovenia   3-2   26/04/2000   (held for two games)

Clubs : Platense, Monaco, Juventus, Hercules, Baniyas, River Plate, Newell's Old Boys, Pune City
International Caps/Goals : - 71/34

Trezeguet would begin his career in Argentina, where he grew up, despite being born in France. Trezeguet spent much of his playing time in the shadow of the more successful Henry, who he would play with at Monaco, Juventus and for the national team. He would remain at Juventus following their relegation to Serie B, adding that title to two Serie A titles, two Ligue 1 titles with Monaco and, like Henry, World Cup 1998 and Euro 2000. It is said that Trezeguet's shot against Manchester United in the 1998 Champions League Quarter Final is the fastest in the history of the tournament in terms of kilometres per hour (157.3km/h)

346. Youri Djorkaeff France (27)
France vs Japan 2-2 04/06/2000

Clubs : Grenoble, Strasbourg, Monaco, Paris Saint Germain, Inter Milan, Kaiserslautern, Bolton Wanderers, Blackburn Rovers, New York Red Bulls
International Caps/Goals : - 28/2

Djorkaeff is of Armenian descent and currently works for charitable organisations in the region. Another member of the World Cup 98 and Euro 2000 winning squads, Djorkaeff would also win the European Cup Winners Cup and UEFA Cup in his career. Later in his career, Djorkaeff joined th' Galacticos at Bolton Wanderers along with Jay-Jay Okocha and Ivan Campo.

347. Sylvain Wiltord France (28,29)
France vs Morocco   5-1   06/06/2000 (held for
two games)

Clubs : Rennes, Deportivo La Coruna, Bordeaux,
Arsenal, Lyon, Marseille, Metz, Nantes
International Caps/Goals : - 92/26

Wiltord would only form part of the Euro 2000
winning French side, not winning a cap for France
until 1999. He would win the French league four
times, and the English Premier League twice.
Wiltord would narrowly avoid death whilst taking
part in a French reality show in 2015, being
eliminated from the show shortly before a
helicopter crash killed three contestants.[xxvi]

348. Youri Djorkaeff France (30)
France vs Czech Republic   2-1   16/06/2000

See Entry 346

349. Bolo Zenden   Netherlands (9)

Netherlands vs France   2-1   21/06/2000

Clubs : PSV, Barcelona, Chelsea, Middlesbrough,
Liverpool, Marseille, Sunderland
International Caps/Goals : - 54/7

Zenden would appear in the Dutch squads that reached two European Championship semi finals and a World Cup semi final during his career, and would win La Liga and Eredivisie. Zenden has been a black belt in judo since the age of 14, following in the footsteps of his father who set up his own dojo in Maastricht.

350. Savo Milosevic — Yugoslavia (12)
Yugoslavia vs Netherlands 1-6 — 25/06/2000

Clubs : Partizan, Aston Villa, Zaragoza, Parma, Espanyol, Celta, Osasuna Rubin Kazan
International Caps/Goals : - 102/37

Milosevic would represent Yugoslavia, Serbia and Montenegro and Serbia in his international career, all three being deemed the successor of the others. The pinnacle of his career (a League Cup with Aston Villa aside) would be securing the Golden Boot at Euro 2000. This 90th minute consolation against the Netherlands in the quarter final, scoring a follow up from a beautiful volley crashing off the bar from Predrag Mijatovic, would be his fifth of the tournament.

352. Predrag Mijatovic — Yugoslavia (13)

Yugoslavia vs Northern Ireland — 2-1 — 16/08/2000

See Entry 325

353. Slavisa Jokanovic   Yugoslavia (14)

Yugoslavia vs Luxembourg   2-0   03/09/2000

Clubs : Novi Sad, Vojvodina, Partizan, Oviedo, Tenerife, Deportivo La Coruna, Chelsea, Ciudad Murcia

International Caps / Goals : - 64/10

Jokanovic would win the Yugoslav First League twice, with Vojvodina and Partizan, however would leave for Spain when war broke out. Whilst in Spain, he would be part of the Deportivo side which won La Liga in the year 2000. Jokanovic would represent Yugoslavia in the 1998 World Cup and Euro 2000.

355. Zlatko Zahovic   Slovenia (1)

Slovenia vs Yugoslavia   1-1   28/03/2001

Slovenia's First 'Last Goal Wins' Trophy

Clubs: Partizan, Proleter Zrenjanin, Vitoria Guimaraes, Porto, Olympiacos, Valencia, Benfica, Limbus Pekre

International Caps/Goals : -   80/35

Perhaps the most notable Slovene footballer pre-indeendence, Zahovic was a key part in his team's qualification for Euro 2000 and World Cup 2002. Following a substitution in Slovenia's group stage defeat against Spain, he would be sent home for insulting Slovenia's coach. A successful career in Portugal would see him win four titles.

356. Ebbe Sand   Denmark (3)

Denmark vs Slovenia   3-0   25/04/2001

Clubs : Brondby, Schalke 04
International Caps/Goals : - 66/22

Sand's goal against Nigeria in the 1998 World Cup would come just 16 seconds after entering the field of play. He would also represent Denmark in the 2002 World Cup and Euro 2000 and 2004. At Brondby, he would the Danish league three times and upon joining Schalke would be top scorer in the Bundesliga in the 2000-2001 season.

357. Jon Dahl Tomasson   Denmark (4)
Denmark vs Czech Republic   2-1   02/06/2001

Clubs : Koge, Heerenveen, Newcastle United, Feyenoord, Milan, Vfb Stuttgart, Villarreal
International Caps/Goals : - 112/52

Along with Tist Nielsen, Tomasson is the top scorer in the history of the Danish national team and would represent them at four international tournaments from Euro 2000 to World Cup 2010. Tomasson would win the UEFA Cup and Champions League in consecutive seasons with Feyenoord and then AC Milan.

358. Ebbe Sand   Denmark (5)
Denmark vs Malta   3-1   06/06/2001

See Entry 356

359. Robert Pires   France (31)
France vs Denmark 1-0   15/08/2001

Clubs : Metz, Marseille, Arsenal, Villarreal, Aston Villa, Goa
International Caps/Goals : - 79/14

Pires is the penultimate player who won both the World Cup in 1998 and Euro 2000 with France to win the 'Last Goal Wins' Trophy (Thierry Henry would win again in 2006). Domestically, Pires would win two league titles with Arsenal, leaving the club in 2006 following their Champions League final defeat, where he was withdrawn after 18 minutes following the dismissal of Jens Lehmann.

360. Reinaldo Navia   Chile (20)

Chile vs France   2-1   01/09/2001

Clubs : Santiago Wanderers, Teco UAG, Monarcas Morelia, America, Monterrey, San Luis, Atlas, Racing Club, LDU Quito, Santiago Morning, Irapuato, Nublense, Atlanta Silverbacks
International Caps/Goals : - 40/10

Navia would be part of the Chile team which would win bronze in the Sydney Olympics in the year 2000. His time in Mexico would see him win one Mexican league title and also be fined $180,000 following an altercation where he claimed he and six of his teammates were mocked by the opposing team, Sao Caetono.

361. Juan Arango Venezuela (1)

Venezuela vs Chile 2-0   04/09/2001

Venezuela's First 'Last Goal Wins' Trophy

Clubs : Nueva Cadiz, Zulia, Caracas, Monterrey, Pachuca, Puebla, Mallorca, Borussia Monchengladbach, Tijuana, New York Cosmos
International Caps/Goals : 129/23

Arango is the record cap holder and record goal scorer for the Venezuelan national team and has appeared in six Copa America tournaments for his country. The only trophy in his career would be the Concacaf Champions League with Pachuca in 2004.

362. Ruberth Moran Venezuela (2)
Venezuela vs Peru   3-0   06/10/2001

Clubs : Estudiantes de Merida, Mineven, Atletico Zulia, Cordoba, Italchacao, Deportivo Tachira, Maracaibo, Atletico Bucaramanga, Argentinos Juniors, Odd Grenland, Cucuta Deportivo
International Caps/Goals : - 65/15

Moran is the fourth highest scorer for the Venezuelan national team, starting his international career in 1996 against Guatemala. The sole title in his long career which took in many clubs across South America, and short stays in Spain and Norway would be in 2008 with Deportivo Tachira in Venezuela.

363. Hector Gonzalez Venezuela (3)
Venezuela vs Paraguay   3-1   08/11/2001

Clubs : Mineros de Guayana, Carabobo, Caracas FC, Olimpo de Bahia Blanca, Colon de Santa Fe, Quilmes, Deportivo Cuenca, LDU Quito, AEK Larnaca, Chernomorets Burgas, Alki Larnaca, Ermis Aradippoy, Llaneros, Atletico Venezuela, Doxa Katokopias, Alki Oroklini, P.O Xylotymbou, ASIL Lysi
International Caps/Goals : - 53/4

Gonzalez is still playing at the age of 44 for ASIL Lysi, a Cypriot team based in Larnaca as Lysi is in Turkish occupied Cyprus. His first move to Europe would be in 2006 at the age of 31, and although he returned to Venezuela for short spells, has played for several further clubs in the Cypriot leagues.

364. Rivaldo   Brazil (25)

Brazil vs Venezuela 3-0   14/11/2001

Clubs : Santa Cruz, Mogi Mirim, Corinthians, Palmeiras, Deportivo, Barcelona, Milan, Cruzeiro, Olympiacos, AEK Athens, Bunyodkor, Sao Paulo, Kabuscorp, Sao Caetano
International Caps/Goals : - 74/35

Rivaldo would win the World Cup in 2002 with Brazil, forming part of a strike force including Ronaldo and Ronaldinho. A total of nine league titles in Brazil, Greece, Spain and Uzbekistan can be added to his 1999 Ballon d'or, which only emphasises the achievements of a player still physically scarred by his upbringing in one of the poorest favelas of Recife. He would retire at the age of 43 having played domestically on four different continents.

365. Ronaldinho   Brazil (26)

Brazil vs Portugal   1-1   17/04/2002

Clubs : Gremio, Paris Saint Germain, Barcelona, Milan, Flamengo, Atletico Mineiro, Queretaro, Fluminense
International Caps/Goals : - 97/33

The second of the three R's (Rivaldo, Ronaldo and Ronaldinho) to win the award, Ronaldinho is considered one of the greatest players of his generation and in history. A key part of Barcelona's Champions League winning side of 2006 setting the foundations for their tiki taka revolution and also a World Cup winner in 2002, Ronaldinho is remembered fondly for playing the game with a smile on his face and an immense amount of skill and quality. Despite scoring many fantastic goals, this equaliser in a friendly against Portugal was a penalty fired into the corner.

2002 – 2016
Modern Day Legends (And Dirk Kuyt)

In 2002, Ronaldo (the original Brazilian one) simply couldn't stop scoring and would hold the title for several consecutive games, the most consecutive title defences in the history of the competition. Two more South American sides would gain the trophy in Paraguay and Venezuela, leaving Ecuador as the only side from the continent yet to win. The early 2010s would see the title rest in the Balkans with Bulgaria and the newly independent Montenegro holding on to the title for several consecutive periods. Finally, it would return to the traditional powerhouses of the European game, and to Santi Cazorla, the titleholder in recess.

Countries

Brazil
Paraguay
Peru
Chile
Venezuela
Norway
Greece
France
Argentina

Switzerland
Netherlands
Romania
Bulgaria
Montenegro
England
Germany
Italy
Spain

Players

366.Luizao   Brazil (27)

Brazil vs Yugoslavia   1-0   27/03/2002

Clubs : Guarani, Parana, Palmeiras, Deportivo La
Coruna, Vasco Da Gama, Corinthians, Gremio,
Hertha Berlin, Botafogo, Sao Paulo, Nagoya
Grampus Eight, Santos, Flamengo, Sao Caetano
International Caps / Goals : 12/4

This would be Luizao's last goal for Brazil, a header
from the six yard box following a failed clearance.
He would form part of the squad that won the
World Cup in 2002. Luizao is also one of few
players to have represented all four of Sao Paulo's
major clubs – Santos, Palmeiras, Corinthians and
Sao Paulo.

367.Edilson   Brazil (28)

Brazil vs Malaysia   4-0   25/05/2002

Clubs : Industrial, Tanabi, Guarani, Palmeiras,
Benfica, Kashiwa Reysol, Corinthians, Flamengo,
Cruzeiro, Vitoria, Al Ain, Sao Caetano, Vasco da
Gama, Nagoya Grampus, Bahia, Taboao da Serra
International Caps/Goals : - 21/6

Edilson is another forward who would have the
misfortune of developing at the time of Ronaldo,
Ronaldinho and Rivaldo (not to mention Adriano,
Djalminha, Luizao), he would however, make two
subsititue appearances in Brazil's World Cup
winning side of 2002. He would be named the best
player, winning the Golden Ball, at the inaugural
Club World Cup whilst at Corinthians.

368.Ronaldo   Brazil (29)

Brazil vs China   4-0   08/06/2002

Clubs : Cruzeiro, PSV, Barcelona, Inter Milan, Real
Madrid, Milan, Corinthians
International Caps/Goals : 98/62

Ronaldo was known as 'the phenomenon' (O Fenomeno in Portuguese) and his astounding goalscoring record throughout his career fits the name. He would win the World Cup in 1994 and 2002 and appear in the final in 1998, a final overshadowed by his convulsive fit in the hours before kick off. In 2006, he would become the top goalscorer in World Cup history (since overtaken by Miroslav Klose). Injury would hamper his career and perhaps negate his full potential, but that Ronaldo could play for rivals Barcelona and Real Madrid, Internazionale and Milan and face little backlash for it is testament to his talent and ability. He is currently the majority owner of Vallodolid in La Liga. This goal would be one of eight in World Cup 2002, a tap in inside the six yard box.

369.Junior   Brazil (30)

Brazil vs Costa Rica 5-2   13/06/2002

Clubs : Vitoria, Palmeiras, Parma, Siena, Sao Paulo, Atletico Mineiro, Goias
International Caps/Goals : - 22/1

The only goal of Junior's Brazil career would come in the final group game of Brazil's 2002 World Cup triumph. Junior would struggle to cement a place in the Brazil side at left back due to the ever presence of Roberto Carlos. Gaining a rare start in this game, Junior would latch onto a through ball on the left wing and place the ball between the keeper and his near post.

370.Nelson Cuevas Paraguay (1,2,3,4)

Paraguay's First Golden Goal

Paraguay vs Brazil   1-0   21/08/2002 (held for 4 games)

Clubs : Sport Colombia, Tembetary, River Plate, Inter Shanghai, Pachuca, Club America, Libertad, Santos, Universidad de Chile, Olimpia Asuncion, Albacete, Puebla, Cerro Porteno, Sportivo Luqueno, Sportivo Carapegua
International Caps/Goals : - 41/6

Three consecutive nil-nil draws would see Cuevas hold the title for a total of four matches. He would represent Paraguay in the 2002 and 2006 World Cups, scoring in both tournaments. He would win titles in Argentina, Mexico, Chile and his native Paraguay.

371.Jefferson Farfan   Peru (9)

Peru vs Paraguay   4-1   06/09/2003

Clubs : Alianza Lima, PSV, Schalke 04, Al Jazira, Lokomotiv Moscow

International Caps/Goals : - 90/26

Perhaps the most notable Peruvian footballer of this century, Farfan would continue his international career to appear in the 2018 World Cup, their first appearance for 36 years. His time in Netherlands would be productive, winning four Eredivisie titles with PSV to add to this three Peruvian titles and a Russian Premier League later on in his career.

372.Arturo Norambuena   Chile (21)

Chile vs Peru 2-1   09/09/2003

Clubs : - Iberia, Santiago Morning, Universidad de Concepcion, Audax Italiano, Universidad Catolica, Quilmes, Cobreloa, Puerto Rico Islanders
International Caps/Goals : 5/1

Norambuena would score his only international goal in this World Cup Qualifier rising above the goalkeeper and defence to nod in a free kick in the 70th minute. He would win two end of season titles in Chile and is now working in the forestry industry.

373.Adrian Romero   Uruguay (22)

Uruguay vs Chile   2-1   15/11/2003

Clubs : Cerro, Nacional Montevideo, Estudiantes de La Plata, Tiro Federal, Queretaro, Olimpia Ascuncion, Cerro Largo, Miramar Misiones

International Caps/Goals : - 8/1

Romero would remain in South America throughout his career, winning titles in both Uruguay and Paraguay, and also playing in Argentina. Romero would climb to win the ball over the Chilean goalkeeper to give Uruguay an important victory in World Cup qualifying.

374.Ronaldo   Brazil (31,32,33,34,35)

Brazil vs Uruguay   3-3   18/11/2003 (held for 5 games)

See Entry 368

375.Reinaldo Navia   Chile (22,23,24)

 Chile vs Brazil   1-1   06/06/2004 (held for 3 games)

See Entry 360.

376.Miguel Villalta   Peru (10)

Peru vs Chile 3-1   18/08/2005

Clubs : Cienciano, Sporting Cristal, Juan Aurich, Melgar, Jose Galvez, Atletico Minero
International Caps/Goals : - 28/2

Playing for Sporting Cristal and Cienciano in three separate spells for both clubs would not bring Villalta domestic glory, but he would appear in the 2007 Copa America for Peru, and win the friendly Kirin Cup in 2005.

377.Jose Torrealba   Venezuela (4)

Venezuela vs Peru   4-1   03/09/2005

Clubs: Universidad de Los Andes, Estudiantes de Merida, Deportivo Tachira, UA Maracaibo, Mamelodi Sundowns, Kaizer Chiefs, Mineros de Guayana, Carabobo. Deportivo Lara, Metropolitanos FC, Trujillanos FC
International Caps/Goals : - 17/4

Torrealba would appear in the Copa America as a subsitute on two occasions in 2007 for Venezuela. He would win two Venezuelan league titles and two South African titles in his career, having played for two clubs in South Africa. Torrealba would lift this over the keeper having been put through in the 79th minute for his second of the game.

378.Nelson Valdez   Paraguay (5,6)

Paraguay vs Venezuela   1-0   08/10/2005 (held for 2 games)

Clubs : Tembetary, Werder Bremen, Borussia Dortmund, Hercules, Rubin Kazan, Valencia, Al Jazira, Olympiacos, Eintracht Frankfurt, Seattle Sounders, Cerro Porteno

International Caps/Goals : - 77/13

Valdez would represent Paraguay in the 2006 and 2010 World Cups and also form part of the squad which finished as runners up in the 2011 Copa America despite not winning a game (two knockout games were won on penalties). Valdez continues to support his home village financially with his wages in European footballer, and once ran into a burning house to save his dog and also chased off car thieves with a shotgun.[xxvii]

379.Frode Johnsen   Norway (1,2)

Norway vs Paraguay   2-2   24/05/2006 (held for 2 games)

Norway's First 'Last Goal Wins' Trophy

Clubs : Odd, Rosenborg, Nagoya Grampus, Shimzu S-Pulse
Internatinoal Caps/ Goals : - 35/10

Johnsen would win six titles with Rosenborg during his time there, and finish as the top scorer in the Norwegian Premier League on three occassions, the latest in 2013 at the age of 39. This form late on in his career would earn him a recall to the Norwegian squad, becoming Norway's oldest ever player in the process.

380.Steffen Iversen Norway (3)
Norway vs Moldova   2-0   06/09/2006

Clubs : Rosenborg, Tottenham Hotspur, Wolverhampton Wanderers, Valerenga, Crystal Palace, Herd, SK Haugar.
International Caps/Goals : - 79/21

Iversen would win six Norwegian titles also, all but one coming for Rosenborg and a League Cup in England with Spurs. He remains the only ever Norwegian goal scorer in a European Championship, scoring against Spain in Euro 2000.

381.Konstantinos Katsouranis   Greece (4,5)

Greece   vs Norway   1-0   07/10/2006 (held
for 2 games)

Clubs : Panachaiki, AEK Athens, Benfica,
Panathinaikos, PAOK, Pune City, Atromitos,
Heidelberg United

Interntional Caps/Goals : - 116/10

Katsouranis's major triumph would come in the
shock victory for Greece in Euro 2004, he would
also appear for Greece in four further international
tournaments including two World Cups. He would
be named Greek footballer of the year in both 2005
and 2013 and win titles in his native country and
Portugal.

382. Thierry Henry France (32)
France vs Greece   1-0   15/11/2006

See Entry 348

383.Javier Saviola   Argentina (24)

Argentina vs France1-0   07/02/2007

Clubs : River Plate, Barcelona, Monaco, Sevilla, Rale
Madrid, Benfica, Malaga, Olympiacos, Verona

International Caps / Goals : - 39/11

Saviola is a player who would not quite live up to his early promise, having won South American Footballer of the year in 1999 at the age of just 18, perhaps slightly burdened by the 'next Maradona' tag hung round him from an early age. He would win a UEFA cup at Sevilla and a Copa Libertadores in 2015 at River Plate towards the end of his career.

384.Marco Streller   Switzerland (13)

Switzerland vs Argentina   1-1   02/06/2007

Clubs : FC Basel, Concordia Basel, FC Thun, VfB Stuttgart
International Caps/Goals : - 37/12

Streller would win eight Swiss titles at FC Basel, sandwiching a single Bundesliga title at Stuttgart. He would miss the final spot kick in the World Cup 2nd Round against Ukraine in the 2006 World Cup, possibly the most boring knockout game in World Cup history.

385.Dirk Kuyt   Netherlands (10)

Netherlands vs Switzerland   1-2   22/08/2007

Clubs : Quick Boys, Utrecht, Feyenoord, Liverpool, Fenerbahce.
International Caps/Goals : - 104/24

A hardworking, industrious winger and striker, Kuyt would never quite reach the heights of some of his contemporaries (Robben, Schneijder, Van Persie) but would be a respected player wherever he went. A runner up in both the World Cup and Champions League, he would win the Eredivisie on his return to Feyenoord at the age of 36.

386.Ruud van Nistelrooy   Netherlands (11)

Netherlands vs Albania   1-0   12/09/2007

Clubs : Den Bosch, Heerenveen, PSV Eindhoven, Manchester United, Real Madrid, Hamburg, Malaga
International Caps/Goals : - 70/35

A prolific goalscorer at both club and international level, van Nistelrooy would represent some of the top European Clubs, winning titles in the Netherlands, England and Spain. His time at Manchester United saw him score 150 goals, 149 of them coming from inside the box. He remains United's second top scorer in European competitions.

387.Dorin Goian   Romania (3)

Romania vs Netherlands   1-0   13/10/2007

Clubs : Foresta Falticeni, Gloria Buzau, Ceahlaul
Piatra Neamt, Bacau, Steaua Bucharest, Palermo,
Rangers, Spezia, Asteras Tripoli
International Caps/Goals : - 60/5

Goian would spend much of his career in his native
Romania despite being consistently linked with
moves to the bigger European leagues. Smashing in
from the rebound following a headed attempt
would be enough to secure victory against the
Netherlands and help ensure Romania's
qualification for Euro 2008.

388.Ciprian Marica   Romania (4)

Romania vs Luxembourg   2-0   17/10/2007

Clubs : Dinamo Bucharest, Shakthar Donetsk, VfB
Stuttgart, Schalke 04, Getafe, Konyaspor, FCSB
International Caps/Goals : 69/25

Marica would also form part of the Euro 2008
squad, along with Dorin Goian. His most
productive period in his career came at Shakhtar
Donetsk, winning two Ukrainian titles and a
Ukrainian Cup. Marica would nearly miss from two
yards out here, just missing the returning
goalkeeper when passing the ball into the net from a
low cross.

389.Velizar Dimitrov   Bulgaria (1)
Bulgaria vs Romania   1-0   17/11/2007

Bulgaria's First 'Last Goal Wins' Trophy

Clubs : Minyor Pernik, Lokomotiv Sofia, Marek
Dupnitsa, CSKA Sofia, Metallurg Donetsk
International Caps/Goals : - 31/4

Dimitrov would represent Bulgaria in Euro 2004,
coming from the bench in two of their fixtures. He
would win three Bulgarian titles and finish as
runner up in the Ukrainian Cup twice. Dimitrov's
header into the roof of the net, is all that would
separate Bulgaria and Romania in a fiesty encounter
in Euro 2008 qualifying.

390.Dimitar Berbatov   Bulgaria (2,3,4)

Bulgaria vs Slovenia   2-0   21/11/2007 (held
for 3 games)

Clubs : CSKA Sofia, Bayer Leverkusen, Tottenham
Hotspur, Manchester United, Fulham, Monaco,
PAOK, Kerala Blasters
International Caps/Goals : - 78/48

The leading goalscorer for the Bulgarian national team, Berbatov would come to prominence as part of the Bayer Leverkusen side which reached the Champions League final in 2002, coming on as a substitute in the fixture himself. Berbatov would spend eight years playing in England, where success with Manchester United would see him win two league titles and the Premier League golden boot.

391.Blagoy Georgiev　　　　　Bulgaria (5,6,7)

Bulgaria vs Montenegro　　2-2　　06/09/2008 (held for 3 games)

Clubs : Slavia Sofia, Deportivo Alaves, Red Star Belgrade, MSV Duisburg, Terek Grozny, Amkar Perm, Rubin Kazan, Orenburg
International Caps/Goals : - 50/5

Geogiev would continue Bulgaria's stranglehold on the title, with a nil-nil draw and the consolation in a thrashing against Serbia. He would spend much of his career in the Russian Federation before retiring in 2017 following an unsuccessful season with Orenburg.

392.Benjamin Huggel　　　　　Switzerland (14)

Switzerland vs Bulgaria　　1-1　　11/02/2009

Clubs : FC Basel, Eintracht Frankfurt
International Caps/Goals : 41/2

Both of Huggel's international goals would be 'Last Goal Wins' title winners, with his goal against Luxembourg being the 1,000[th] international goal for Switzerland. Spending his career largely at the dominant FC Basel, he would win seven titles for the club and five Swiss cups.

393.Gelson Fernandes   Switzerland (15,16)

Switzerland vs Moldova   2-0   28/03/2009 (held for 2 games)

Clubs : Sion, Manchester City, Saint Etienne, Chievo, Leicester, Udinese, Sporting Lisbon, SC Freiburg, Rennes, Eintracht Frankfurt
International Caps/Goals : - 67/2

Fernandes was originally born in Cape Verde, moving to Switzerland at the age of five and first representing the Swiss national team in 2007. His other goal for Switzerland would be the winner in a defensive victory of eventual winners Spain in the 2010 World Cup group stages. He would win the Swiss and German Cups during his career.

394.Marco Padolino
          Switzerland (17)

Switzerland vs Greece   2-0   05/09/2009

Clubs : Lugano, Malcantone Agno, Catania, Piacenza, Sampdoria, Vicenza
International Caps/Goals : - 9/1

Padolino would form part of the the Swiss World Cup 2010 squad, this being his only international goal in the 87th minute with a diving header to assist in qualification for the tournament. His last appearance for the Swiss national team would be in August 2010.

395.Eren Derdiyok   Switzerland (18)

Switzerland vs Latvia   2-2   09/09/2009

Clubs : Old Boys, FC Basel, Bayer Leverkusen, 1899 Hoffenheim, Kasimpas, Galatasaray
International Caps/Goals : - 60/11

Representing Switzerland in Euro 2008 (where he was the youngest player), World Cup 2010 and Euro 2016, Derdiyok has been a part of the Swiss national team for over a decade, the highlight of his international career being a hattrick against Germany in 2012. Domestically, he has won titles in Switzerland and Turkey ten years apart in 2008 and 2018 respectively.

396.Benjamin Huggel   Switzerland (19)

Switzerland vs Luxembourg   3-0   10/10/2009

See Entry 392.

397.John Carew   Norway (4)

Norway vs Switzerland   1-0   14/11/2009

Clubs : Valerenga, Rosenborg, Valencia, Roma, Besiktas, Lyon, Aston Villa, Stoke City, West Ham United
International Caps/Goals : - 91/24

Carew is perhaps best known for his time at Valencia where his excellent hold up play and ability as a target man would help them to the 2001-2002 La Liga title and miss out on the Champions League in 2002 on penalties (although Carew would score his penalty in the final shootout). His penalty in this international friendly against Switzerland would end an unbeaten run of eleven games for the Swiss national team.

398.Mirko Vucinic   Montenegro (1)

Montenegro vs Norway   1-2   29/05/2010

Montenegro's First 'Last Goal Wins' Trophy

Clubs : Sutjeska Niksic, Lecce, Roma, Juventus, Al Jazira
International Caps/Goals : - Serbia and Montenegro 3/0 Montenegro 45/17

Perhaps the most significant footballer available to Montenegro following their independence from Serbia, he would score their first international goal and be their top international goalscorer until overtaken by Stefan Jovetic in 2016.

399.Radomir Djalovic   Montenegro (2)

Montenegro vs Northern Ireland 2-0   11/08/2010

Clubs : Jedinstvo Bijelo Polje, Red Star Belgrade, Zeleznik, Zagreb, Armini Bielefeld, Kayseri Erciyesspor, Rijeka, Rapid Bucharest, Amkar Perm, Sepahan, Shanghai Shenxin, BEC Tero Sasana, Bangkok, Buducnost, Rudar Pljevlja
International Caps/Goals : - 22/7

Djalovic has had something of a nomadic football career starting at his hometown club in Montenegro before taking in clubs in Serbia, Croatia, Germany, Turkey, Romania, Russia, Iran, China and Thailand. He would make his final appearance for Montenegro in 2012.

400.Mirko Vucinic   Montenegro (3)

Montenegro vs Wales   1-0   03/09/2010

See Entry 398

401.Elsad Zverotic   Montenegro (4)

Montenegro vs Bulgaria   1-0   07/09/2010

Clubs : FC Bazenheid, FC Wil, FC Luzern, Young
Boys, Fulham, Sion, Aarau
International Caps / Goals : - 61/5

Zverotic continues to play for Montenegro where he
is the current record holder for international caps.
He did initially represent Switzerland at youth
level. Zverotic's first international goal here, would
see him hit a low strike into the bottom corner via
the post from around twenty five metres.

402.Mirko Vucinic   Montenegro (5)
Montenegro vs Switzerland   1-0   08/10/2010

See Entry 398

403.Ivelin Popov   Bulgaria (8)

Bulgaria vs Montenegro   1-1   04/06/2011

Clubs : Litex Lovech, Gaziantepspor, Kuban
Krasnodar, Spartak Moscow, Rostov
International Caps/Goals : - 82/14

Popov is a controversial figure in Bulgarian football known for his temperament along with his footballing skills. He has been banned on three separate occasions by the Bulgarian Football Association, including a life ban which has since been overturned.[xxviii]

404.Wayne Rooney England (51)

England vs Bulgaria   3-0   02/09/2011

Clubs : Everton, Manchester United, DC United

International Caps/Goals : - 120/53

England's record goalscorer, Rooney is another who has faced questions regarding his temperament throughout his career since making his debut at 16 for Everton. During his time with Manchester United, Rooney won every single trophy available to him with the exception of the European Super Cup, including in that spell five Premier League titles. He would represent England in three World Cups and three European Championships in his career.

405.Ashley Young England (52)

England vs Wales   1-0   06/09/2011

Clubs : Watford, Aston Villa, Manchester United

International Caps/Goals : - 39/7

Young began his career as a winger and has slowly developed into a full back at Manchester United wining a recall to the England squad after a four year absence following Euro 2012. He formed part of the England squad which finished 4th in the 2018 World Cup and has won every competition in domestic English football.

406.Andrija Delibasic   Montenegro (6)

Montenegro vs England   2-2   07/10/2011

Clubs : Partizan, Mallorca, Benfica, Braga, AEK Athens, Beira Mar, Real Sociedad, Hercules, Rayo Vallecano, Ratchaburi, Sutjeska

International Caps/Goals : - 20/6

Delibasic would form part of Benfica's title winning side in 2004/2005 whilst on loan from Mallorca. Delibasic's 90th minute headed equaliser would secure a famous point at home for Montenegro, having come from two goals down against England.

407.Stephan Lichtsteiner
          Switzerland (20,21)

Switzerland vs Montenegro   2-0   11/10/2011
(held for 2 games)

Clubs : Grasshoppe, Lille, Lazio, Juventus, Arsenal
International Caps/Goals : - 105/8

Lichtsteiner would win seven titles in a row whilst
at Juventus, adding four Italian cups in the same
spell. Having gained over a hundred caps for
Switzerland, he is currently the third highest
capped Swiss footballer, appearing in three World
Cups and two European Championships.

408.Granit Xhaka   Switzerland (22)

Switzerland vs Luxembourg   1-0   15/11/2011

Clubs : Basel, Borussia Monchengladbach, Arsenal
International Caps/Goals : - 74/11

Current Arsenal teammate of Lichtsteiner, Xhaka
would take the title in a 1-0 win against
Luxembourg. Coming from Albanian descent,
Xhaka would take to the field against his brother
Taulant in Switzerland's opening Euro 2016 fixture
against Albania. Whilst at Basel, he would win two
Swiss titles and also formed part of the Swiss side
who would the under 17 World Cup in 2009.

409.Lionel Messi   Argentina (25)

Argentina vs Switzerland   3-1   29/02/2012

Clubs : Barcelona
International Caps/Goals : -129/65

Widely regarded as one of the greatest footballers in
history and, along with Cristiano Ronaldo, has
dominated world football through the late 2000s to
the present day. Messi holds multiple individual
records including the most goals scored in La Liga
both all time and in a single season. Whereas
domestically, Messi has won almost every honour
available to him, including nine La Liga titles and
four Champions League, he has not been able to
replicate that at international level, finishing as
runner up in the 2014 World Cup and the 2007, 2015
and 2016 Copa Americas.

410.Angel di Maria   Argentina (26)

Argentina vs Ecuador   4-0   02/06/2012

Clubs : Rosario Central, Benfica, Real Madrid,
Manchester United, Paris Saint Germain

International Caps/Goals : - 97/20

Di Maria would form part of the Argentina under 20 World Cup winning side and the Olympic Games in 2008. Di Maria has won titles in Portugal, Spain and France and a Champions League with Real Madrid. The fourth goal in a demolition of Ecuador in the qualifiers for the 2014 World Cup would see Di Maria hit a low half volley into the bottom corner.

411.Lionel Messi   Argentina (27)

Argentina vs Brazil 4-3   09/06/2012

See Entry 409

412.Benedikt Howedes   Germany (8,9)

Germany vs Argentina   1-3   15/08/2012 (held for 2 games)

Clubs : Schalke 04, Juventus, Lokomotiv Moscow

International Caps/Goals : - 44/2

Howedes would play in every minute of Germany's successful 2014 World Cup campaign, and this represented his first international goal. Domestically, Howedes spent much of his career with Schalke, winning the German Cup in his time there, a short loan spell at Juventus saw him win the Coppa Italia and Serie A.

413.Sami Khedira   Germany (10)

Germany vs France 2-1   06/02/2013

Clubs : VfB Stuttgart, Real Madrid, Juventus

International Caps/Goals : - 77/7

The second member of Germany's 2014 World Cup winning squad to gain the title, Khedira would like much of his teammates play in their victorious 2009 under 21 European Championship side. Khedira is of Tunisian origin, and has now won three consecutive Serie A titles with Juventus. His winning goal in a friendly in the Stade de France would see him calmly slot the ball past the onrushing keeper from inside the box.

414.Thomas Muller   Germany (11)

Germany vs Kazakhstan 3-0   22/03/2013

Clubs : Bayern Munich

International Caps/Goals : 100/38

Having been at Munich all of his career, Muller has won, seven Bundesliga titles and one Champions League to add to his World Cup with Germany in 2014. He came to prominence in the 2010 World Cup, where his five goals would be sufficient to secure the Golden Boot, securing another five in the 2014 World Cup.

415.Marco Reus   Germany (12)

Germany vs Kazakhstan   4-1   26/03/2013

Clubs : Rot Weiss Ahlen, Borussia Monchengladbach, Borussia Dortmund
International Caps/Goals : - 39/10

Reus would miss the 2014 World Cup with an ankle injury in the warm up to the tournament, other injuries have stunted his career, although he would appear in the 2018 World Cup. In 2014, Reus would be fined €540,000 for driving with a fake licence, although he has since passed his driving test.[xxix]

416.Lars Bender   Germany (13)

Germany vs Paraguay   3-3   14/08/2013

Clubs : 1860 Munich, Bayer Leverkusen

International Caps/Goals : 19/4

Bender would also miss out on the 2014 World Cup victory through injury, despite having been called up to the provisional squad. He would have the opportunity to make amends, being selected for the 2016 Olympic Games football tournament where Germany would secure silver. The final of his four international goals, Bender would bring down a clearance onto his chest from the edge of the box, volleying across the goalkeeper and into the far corner.

417.Ignazio Abate Italy (15)

Italy vs Germany   1-1   15/11/2013

Clubs : Milan, Napoli, Piacenza. Modena, Empoli, Torino
International Caps/Goals : 22/1

Abate would have to begin his career away from Milan before returning after two years away to become an integral part of their side and the 2010/2011 Serie A winning team. His only international goal, the equaliser in a friendly against Germany, would see him perform an excellent one-two to move into the box and then placing the ball in off the post.

418.Pedro   Spain (20)

Spain vs Italy   1-0   05/03/2014

Clubs : Barcelona, Chelsea
International Caps/Goals : - 64/17

Pedro would win the World Cup in 2010 and Euro 2012 as part of the Spain team which dominated international football over this period. Five titles at Barcelona can be added to one at Chelsea, and three Champions League winners medals whilst at the Catalan club.

419.Andres Iniesta   Spain (21)

Spain vs Bolivia   2-0   30/05/2014

Clubs : Barcelona, Vissel Kobe
International Caps/Goals : 131/13

Scoring the winning goal in the 2010 World Cup final would be the pinnacle of Iniesta's career but would also be his redemption, coming after a year struggling with injury and depression.[xxx] The World Cup victory would be cemented by two consecutive European Championship wins and a total of 9 La Liga titles and four Champions League trophies.

420.David Villa   Spain (22)

Spain vs El Salvador   2-0   07/06/2014

Clubs : Sporting Gijon, Zaragoza, Valencia, Barcelona, Atletico Madrid, New York City, Melbourne City, Vissel Kobe
International Caps/Goals : - 98/59

Villa would also play an important role in the 2010 World Cup victory and also be a part of the 2008 European Championship side, missing out on 2012 with injury. He remains Spain's top goalscorer, and also has team honours to his name, winning La Liga twice with Barcelona and once with Atletico Madrid.

421.Juan Mata   Spain (23,24)

Spain vs Australia   3-0   23/06/2014 (held for 2 games)

Clubs : Real Madrid, Valencia, Chelsea, Manchester United

International Caps/Goals : - 41/10

For a brief period in his career, Mata was the holder of the latest Champions League, UEFA Cup/Europa League, World Cup and European Championships following Chelsea's successes in 2012 and 2013 in the club game, and Spain's victories internationally. This goal in the 2014 group stage for Spain would still see the World Champions knocked out despite Mata nutmegging the goalkeeper from within the six yard box. Mata's next appearance for Spain in 2015 would see an own goal help him retain the title.

424.Santi Cazorla   Spain (25,26)

Spain vs Luxembourg   4-0   09/10/2015 (held for 2 games, no further appearances for Spain)

Clubs : Villarreal, Recreativo Huelva, Malaga, Arsenal
International Caps/Goals : - 77/14

Cazorla is the current titleholder in recess, having not made an appearance for Spain since 2016 having injured his Achilles tendon, requiring eight operations on his ankle. Further to this he contracted gangrene and required a skin graft on the affected leg. He has since return to Villarreal, where he started his career and has returned to playing.

2016 – ONWARDS.
LITTLE FISHES, SMALL POND

It's worth noting that Santi Cazorla has not officially retired from international football, although his last appearance he did retain the 'Last Goal Wins' Trophy. This represents a divergence in the potential winners Cazorla could theoretically return to compete for his title again. The new UEFA Nations League has also meant that, with teams playing their relative peers, once going to the smaller nations in Europe, it has remained with those – who now have more chance of scoring.

Countries

Spain
Georgia
Eire
Iceland
Qatar
Liechtenstein
Andorra
Kazakhstan
Latvia
North Macedonia

Players

425. Aritz Aduriz   (Spain 27,28)

Spain vs Italy   1-1   24/03/2016 (held for
two games)

Clubs : Athletic Bilbao, Burgos, Vallodolid,
Mallorca, Valencia.
International Caps/Goals : - 13/2

A product of the Bilbao youth academy, Aduriz was
a surprise inclusion in the Spain Euro 2016 squad at
the age of 35, having not appeared for Spain since
2010. Aduriz has also represented the Basque
national team.

426. Alvaro Morata   Spain (29)

Spain vs South Korea   6-1   01/06/2016

Clubs : - Real Madrid, Juventus, Chelsea, Atletico
Madrid
International Caps/Goals : - 29/15

Currently on loan at Atletico Madrid from Chelsea,
Morata has won two La Liga titles with their city
rivals Real and also two Champions League titles.
Morata has cost over €100 million in transfer fees
since the start of career, with Real Madrid involved
in all three transfers as either buyer or seller.

427. Tornike Okriashvili   Georgia (1)

Georgia vs Spain   1-0   07/06/2016

Georgia's First 'Last Goal Wins' Trophy

Clubs : Gagra, Shakhtar Donetsk, Illichevets
Mariupol, Chornomorets Odessa, Genk,
Eskisehirspor, Krasnodar
International Caps/Goals : - 36/9

Okriashvili scored the winner in a shock 1-0 victory
for Georgia against Spain prior to the Euro 2016
tournament, meaning that the title would not been
contested in the tournament. He would be
celebrated as Georgian Footballer of the Year in
2016.

428. Jano Ananidze   Georgia (2)

Georgia vs Austria   1-2   05/09/2016

Clubs : Spartak Moscow, Rostov, Krylia Sovetov
Samara
International Caps / Goals : - 48/9

Ananidze became the youngest goal scorer in the
Russian Premier league at 17 years and 8 days old in
October 2009. He would win the Russian Premier
League with Spartak Moscow in 2017 to follow a
Russian Cup with Rostov in 2014.

429. Seamus Coleman   Eire (2)

Eire vs   Georgia   1-0   06/10/2016

Clubs : Sligo Rovers, Everton, Blackpool
International Caps / Goals : - 51/1

Coleman's first international goal would secure a win against Georgia and would suffer a serious leg fracture in a later qualifying fixture against Wales.. His brother participated in the 2003 Special Olympics World Summer Games football competition.

430. James McClean   Eire (3,4,5)

Eire vs Moldova   3-1   09/10/2016 (held for three games)

Clubs : Institute, Derry, Sunderland, Wigan, West Bromwich Albion, Stoke City
International Caps/Goals : 65/10

McLean would hold the 'Last Goal Wins' Trophy for three games, following scoring the winner against Austria in November 2016 and a 0-0 draw against Wales in March 2017. McLean is the subject of much controversy, growing up in Derry, Northern Ireland and refusing to wear a poppy (which commemorates British war dead) due to Derry's troubled history.[xxxi]

431. Hordur Magnusson   Iceland (1,2)

Iceland   vs Ireland   1-0   28/03/2017 (held for two games)

Iceland's First 'Last Goal Wins' Trophy

Clubs : Fram, Juventus, Spezia, Cesena, Bristol City, CSKA Moscow
International Caps/Goals : - 24/2

A skilful free kick lofted over the Irish wall and into the bottom corner would secure a first 'Last Goal Wins' Trophy for Iceland and Magnusson. His second international goal, the winner against Croatia in a World Cup qualification match would also be a 'Last Goal Wins' Trophy.

432. Gylfi Sigurdsson   Iceland (3)

Iceland   vs Ukraine   2-0   05/09/2017

Clubs : Reading, Shrewsbury Town, Crewe Alexandra, 1899 Hoffenheim, Swansea City, Tottenham Hotspur, Everton
International Caps/Goals : 66/20

Seven times Icelandic footballer of the year Sigurdsson has represented the Atlantic island country in the European Championship in 2016 and World Cup in 2018. He has spent much of his career in England, and is the 1st, 3rd and 4th most expensive Icelandic footballer in history.

433. Kari Arnarson   Iceland (4)

Iceland   vs Turkey   3-0   06/10/2017

Clubs : Vikingur, Djurgarden, AGF Aarhus, Esjberg, Plymouth Argyle, Aberdeen, Rotherham United, Malmo, Omonia, Genclerbirligi
International Caps/Goals : - 75/6

Another member of the Icelandic national team's squads in Euro 2016 and World Cup 2018, he has won two Swedish titles in his career eleven years apart. In 2011, Arnason made potentially the longest move available in British football, moving to Aberdeen following his release from Plymouth during the latter's administration.

434. Johann Gudmundsson
       Iceland (5)

Iceland vs Kosovo   2-0   09/10/2017

Clubs : Breidablik, AZ, Charlton Athletic, Burnley
Internationl Caps/Goals : - 72/7

Joining Arnarson and Sigurdsson in Iceland's two tournament appearances, Gudmundsson would assist Iceland's first goal in Euro 2016, and scored the country's first hat trick in 13 years against Switzerland in 2013. His goal here against Kosovo, a shot into the roof of the net within the six yard box would help Iceland qualify for World Cup 2018.

435. Kjartan Finnbogason   Iceland (6)

Iceland   vs Czech Republic 1-2   08/11/2017

Clubs : KR Reykjavik, Celtic, Queens Park, Atvidabergs, Sandjeford, Falkirk, AC Horsens, Ferencvaros, Vejle BK

International Caps/Goals : - 11/2

The first player with an affiliation with Queens Park to win the title for over 100 years, Finnbogason would not make the Icelandic squads for either tournament. This goal would be a header from inside the six yard box past the Czech goalkeeper.

436. Mohammed Muntari   Qatar (1)

Qatar vs Iceland   1-1   14/11/2017

Qatar's First 'Last Goal Wins' Trophy, First 'Last Goal Wins' Trophy in Asia, First 'Last Goal Wins' Trophy outside of Europe/ South America

Clubs : El Jaish, Lekhwiya, Al Duhail, Al Ahli
International Caps/Goals : 17/7

Muntari would score the first 'Last Goal Wins' Trophy for an Asian country in Qatar's friendly against Iceland in November 2017, despite being born and raised in Africa. He became naturalised in Qatar following his residence there from 2013 onwards.

437. Michele Polverino   Liechtenstein (1)

Liechtenstein vs Qatar   2-1   14/12/2017

Liechtenstein's First 'Last Goal Wins' Trophy

Clubs : FC Vaduz, Olbia Calcio, FC Aarau, Steel Azin, Wolfsberger AC, SV Ried, FC Rapperswil-Jona, FC Balzers

International Caps/Goals : - 73/6

Twice a winner of Liechtenstein's player of the year, in 2012 and 2013, Polverino would score the winner in a friendly against Qatar to secure the 'Last Goal Wins' Trophy for himself and the tiny Alpine nation which represented an embarrassing defeat for the future World Cup hosts.

438. Marc Rebes   Andorra (1,2,3,4)

Andorra vs Liechtenstein   1-0   21/03/2018 (held for four games)

Andorra's First 'Last Goal Wins' Trophy

Clubs : FC Santa Coloma
International Caps/Goals : 23/2

Rebes second international goal for Andorra would also come as a winner in a rare victory for the national team, having previously scored the winner against Hungary in 2018 World Cup Qualifying. Three consecutive 0-0 draws against Cape Verde, UAE and Latvia would see Rebes hold the title for 6 months of 2018.

439. Jordi Alaez   Andorra (5)

Andorra vs Kazakhstan   1-1   10/09/2018

Clubs : FC Andorra
International Caps/Goals : - 19/1

Alaez has also played for the Andorra beach soccer team, which is ranked 62nd out of 113 beach soccer teams, making it more successful than the ordinary football team. An 85th minute equaliser following a misplaced backpass by a Kazakh defender, brought Alaez to tears and a rare draw for the Andorran national team.

440. Roman Murtasayev   Kazakhstan (1)

Kazakhstan vs   Andorra   4-0   16/10/2018

Kazakhstan's First 'Last Goal Wins' Trophy

Clubs : Shakhter Karagandy, Irtysh Pavlodar, Astana
International Caps/Goals : 22/3

Murtasayev has spent all of his career in his home country of Kazakhstan, winning two league titles in 2017 and 2018. He would be part of the Astana team who made it to the Europa League round of 16 in 2018.

441. Deniss Rakels   Latvia (1,2)

Latvia vs Kazakhstan   1-1   15/11/2018 (held for two games)

Latvia's First 'Last Goal Wins' Trophy

Clubs : FK Liepajas Metalurgs, Zaglebie Lubin, GKS Katowice, Cracovia, Reading, Lech Poznan, Cracovia, Riga, Pafos

International Caps/Goals : - 28/1

Rakels first international goal succeeded in giving him the 'Last Goal Wins' Trophy, which he would retain in a goalless draw against Andorra in the subsequent UEFA Nations League fixture. His only title is the Virsliga in 2009 with Liepajas Metalurgs.

442. Elif Elmas   North Macedonia (1)

North Macedonia vs Latvia   3-1   21/03/2019

North Macedonia's First 'Last Goal Wins' Trophy

Clubs : Rabotnicki, Fenerbahce

International Caps/Goals : - 10/2

Elmas is of Turkish descent and although rejected a call from Turkey to play for their national side, currently plays his club football in the Turkish Super League. Elmas first international goals would come in this game, the final coming in the 93rd minute to secure the 'Last Goal Wins' Trophy.

443. Enis Bardhi   North Macedonia (2)

North Macedonia vs Slovenia   1-1   24/03/2019

Clubs: Prespa Birlik, Ujpest, Levante

International Caps/Goals : - 21/4

Bardhi is a Macedonian of Albanian descent, although he would allegedly turn down the Albanian national team despite making overtures to them. His equaliser in the Euro 2020 qualifier against Slovenia would see him the current holder of the 'Last Goal Wins' Trophy.

Full Country List

1.England 52
2.Scotland 44
3.Brazil 35
4.France 32
5. Spain 29
6. Argentina 27
7. Chile 24
8. Switzerland 22
9. Uruguay 22
10. Wales 15
11. Italy 15
12. Belgium 14
13. Yugoslavia 14
14. Hungary 13
15. Germany 13
16. Netherlands 11
17. West Germany 11
18. Peru 10
19. Poland 9
20. Bulgaria 8
21. Austria 6
22.Paraguay 6
23. Montenegro 6
24. Iceland 6
25.Ireland 5
26. Eire 5
27. Greece 5
28. Denmark 5

PLAYERS TO HAVE WON MORE THAN TWICE

1. Steve Bloomer - England **(Entry 33)** – 9
2. Ronaldo – Brazil - **(Entry 368)** – 6
3. John O'Hare – Scotland **(Entry 235)** – 5
4. Michel Platini – France **(Entry 263)** – 5
5. Andrew Wilson – Scotland **(Entry 71)** – 4
6. Jean Baratte – France **(Entry 134)** – 4
7. Oscar Miguez – Uruguay **(Entry 148)** – 4
8. Jorge Aravena – Chile **(Entry 278)** – 4
9. Claudio Caniggia – Argentina **(Entry 299)** – 4
10. Nelson Cuevas – Paraguay **(Entry 370)** – 4
11. Reinaldo Navia – Chile **(Entry 360)** – 4
12. Marc Rebes – Andorra **(Entry 418)** – 4
13. Lauro Amado – Switzerland **(Entry 118)** – 3
14. Oscar Gomez Sanchez – Peru **(Entry 161)** – 3
15. Mazzola – Brazil **(Entry 189)** – 3
16. Uwe Seeler – West Germany **(Entry 194)** – 3
17. Nelson Agresta – Uruguay **(Entry 274)** – 3
18. Juan Carlos Letelier – Chile **(Entry 279)** – 3
19. Romario – Brazil **(Entry 300)** – 3
20. Dimitar Berbatov – Bulgaria **(Entry 390)** – 3
21. Blagoy Georgiev – Bulgaria **(Entry 391)** – 3
22. Mirko Vucinic – Montenegro **(Entry 398)** – 3
23. James McLean – Eire **(Entry 430)** - 3

i   The Lost Professional of Everton FC – Tony Onslow
    08/10/2013 – viewed 10/03/2019
    https://www.toffeeweb.com/season/13-
    14/comment/fan/25805.html
ii The Forgotten Story of.... Fred Spiksley – The Guardian
    28/07/2018 viewed 26/03/2019
    https://www.theguardian.com/sport/2017/jul/28/for
    gotten-story-fred-spiksley-simon-burnton
iii The Question: Why is the modern offside law a work
    of genius? The Guardian 13/04/2010 viewed
    13/03/2019
    https://www.theguardian.com/sport/blog/2010/apr/
    13/the-question-why-is-offside-law-genius
iv http://www.rsssf.com/miscellaneous/iffhs-
    century.html
v How Uruguay broke Brazilian hearts in the 1950 World Cup. BBC
News. Viewed 09/02/2019
https://www.bbc.com/news/magazine-27767298
vi Dicconario Biografico Del Futbol Boliviano 1930-2000
    – Delfin Sanchez Seborga p15
    https://repositorio.umsa.bo/bitstream/handle/123456
    789/7119/DICCIONARIO%20BIOGRAFICO%20DEL
    %20FUTBOL%20BOLIVIANO.pdf?
    sequence=2&isAllowed=y
vii Dicconario Biografico Del Futbol Boliviano 1930-2000
    – Delfin Sanchez Seborga p67
    https://repositorio.umsa.bo/bitstream/handle/123456
    789/7119/DICCIONARIO%20BIOGRAFICO%20DEL
    %20FUTBOL%20BOLIVIANO.pdf?
    sequence=2&isAllowed=y
viii Los Dos Guillermo Diaz – La Tercera viewed
    09/02/2019 https://www.latercera.com/noticia/los-
    dos-guillermo-diaz/
ix Fallecio el exfutbolista Roberto 'Tito' Drago – La
    Republica viewed 14/02/2019
    https://larepublica.pe/deportes/829332-fallecio-el-
    exfutbolista-roberto-tito-drago

[x] Omar Sivori – The Telegraph 19/02/2005 – viewed 14/02/2019

https://www.telegraph.co.uk/news/obituaries/1483849/Omar-Sivori.html

[xi] Nota exclusiva con Antonio Garabal, una parte de la historia de Ferro : - http://www.ferroweb.com.ar/verdolag/reportaj/garabal/antonio_garabal.htm

[xii] La tarde en que Sanfilippo 'termino' con su carrera – viewed 18/02/2019

http://www.canaltrans.com/deportes/futbol1/historias/035.html

[xiii] The Battle of Santiago – Ken Pendleton – viewed 09/02/2019
https://ussoccerplayers.com/the-battle-of-santiago

[xiv] Neymar, The Making of the World's Greatest New Number 10 – Luca Caioli (Icon Books 2014)

[xv] Amarildo não é mais o técnico do América – Globosports. 30/01/2008 – viewed 20/02/2019
https://oglobo.globo.com/esportes/amarildo-nao-mais-tecnico-do-america-3850560

[xvi] John Greig, Scotland's Greatest Team – STV 01/04/2010 – viewed 20/02/2019

https://web.archive.org/web/20100406054407/http://sport.stv.tv/greatest-team/players-managers/164241-john-greig/

[xvii] Scotland's Iconic Moments No 46 – Sunday Post viewed 20/02/2019
http://www.sundaypost100.com/2015/10/01/46-rangers-win-european-cup-winners-cup/

[xviii] Obituary: Jimmy Johnstone – The Guardian 14 Mar 2006 viewed 27/02/2019

https://www.theguardian.com/news/2006/mar/14/guardianobituaries.football

xix Rune Hauge, International Man of Mystery – The Guardian 18 March 2000 viewed 28/02/2019

https://www.theguardian.com/football/2000/mar/18/newsstory.sport1

xx The game's terrible twins – Fifa.com 12/02/2010 viewed 02/03/2019 https://www.fifa.com/news/the-game-terrible-twins-1169316

xxi Paul Gascoigne – National Football Museum Hall of Fame – viewed 09/02/2019

https://www.nationalfootballmuseum.com/halloffame/paul-gascoigne/

xxii https://www.tuttomercatoweb.com/le-meteore/perdomo-il-cane-volante-del-genoa-74462 – viewed 14/02/2019 https://www.tuttomercatoweb.com/le-meteore/perdomo-il-cane-volante-del-genoa-74462

xxiii Millwall pull off coup by securing Spartak Pair – The Independent Sat 06 January 1996 – viewed 03/03/2019 https://www.independent.co.uk/sport/millwall-pull-off-coup-by-securing-spartak-pair-1322708.html

xxiv Hajto skazany za śmiertelne potrącenie staruszki – Dziennik Gazeta Prawna 07.06.201 – viewed 03/03/2019 https://sport.dziennik.pl/artykuly/68291,hajto-skazany-za-smiertelne-potracenie-staruszki.html

xxv The 10 Worst Examples of footballers behaving badly – The Observer Sport Monthly, 04 Nov 2001 – viewed 03/03/2019

https://www.theguardian.com/observer/osm/story/0,,583485,00.html

xxvi Former Arsenal Star Sylvain Wiltord Shocked by Argentina Helicopter Crash – The Telegraph 10/03/2015 viewed 04/03/2019

https://www.telegraph.co.uk/sport/football/teams/arsenal/11461360/Former-Arsenal-star-Sylvain-Wiltord-shocked-by-Argentina-helicopter-crash.html

xxvii Nelson Valdez hails a dream come true as Hercules shock Barcelona – Sid Lowe, The Guardian 13-09-2019 – viewed 06/03/2019

https://www.theguardian.com/football/blog/2010/sep/13/hercules-stun-barcelona-sid-lowe

xxviii Enfant terrible Popov comes of age for Bulgaria – Fifa.Com 12/09/2017 – viewed 09/03/2019
https://www.fifa.com/worldcup/news/enfant-terrible-popov-comes-of-age-for-bulgaria-2907629

xxix Marco Reus passes driving test two years after 540,000 euros fine – Michael Kelleher 23/08/2016 – viewed 10/03/2019

https://www.skysports.com/football/news/11899/10538830/marco-reus-passes-driving-test-two-years-after-540000-euros-fine

xxx Barcelona's Andres Iniesta: I was a Victim of something that terrified me – The Guardian 06/09/2016 Sid Lowe – viewed 10/09/2019

https://www.theguardian.com/football/2016/sep/06/barcelona-andres-iniesta-need-help-look-for-it

xxxi James McClean reveals why he won't wear a Remembrance Day poppy on his West Brom shirt – The Mirror 31/10/2015 – viewed 14/02/2019

https://www.mirror.co.uk/sport/football/news/james-mcclean-reveals-wont-wear-6740133

Printed in Poland
by Amazon Fulfillment
Poland Sp. z o.o., Wrocław

51154953R00148